Foster carer reviews
Process, practicalities and best practice

Helen Cosis Brown

Published by CoramBAAF Adoption and Fostering Academy
41 Brunswick Square
London WC1N 1AZ
www.corambaaf.org.uk

First edition published by BAAF 2011
Second edition © Helen Cosis Brown, 2015. Reprinted 2020, 2021

British Library Cataloguing in Publication Data
A catalogue record for this book is available from the British Library
ISBN 978 1 910039 37 3

Designed and typeset by Helen Joubert Design
Printed in Great Britain by the Lavenham Press

Contents

Acknowledgements (2011 edition)

My thanks go to the following people whose advice and knowledge have been invaluable: Hazel Halle, Ruth Richards, Freda Lewis, Frances Nicholson, Phyllis Elwood, Linda Norwood, Diana Searle, Ena Fry, Aaron Brown, Casey Ryan, Rebecca Swift, Meral Mehmet, Sandy Lane, Tammy Desouza, Philippa Williams, Christine Cocker, Philip Sutton, Sarah Lewis-Brooke, Lynn Woodhouse, Sarah Borthwick, Alison King, Joy Howard, Sue Anderson, Kate Alibone, Maureen Ingham and Doreen Price.

I would like to acknowledge the help I have received from the following organisations: the Wales, Scotland, Northern Ireland and London BAAF offices; the Wales, Scotland, Northern Ireland and London Fostering Network offices and the National Society for the Prevention of Cruelty to Children's Library. The staff from these organisations have been models of "good practice".

Particular thanks go to Ena Fry who read the draft Guide manuscript and gave helpful comments and suggestions, Elaine Dibben from BAAF whose comments were invaluable and Shaila Shah for BAAF's editorial support.

Chapters 5 and 6 draw on the model of good practice developed by Greater London Fostering.

Thanks also go to the panel members of the four fostering panels I have chaired since 1998 and to the foster children, foster carers, foster carers' own children, supervising social workers and their managers I have worked with over the years; all of whom have contributed to my thinking about foster carer reviews.

Note to the 2015 edition

This edition has been published by CoramBAAF Adoption and Fostering Academy, a part of the Coram group. This entity was formed in 2015 following a transfer of some services from BAAF (the British Association for Adoption & Fostering) to the Coram group.

Note about the author

Helen Cosis Brown (PhD) (MSW) (BA) (CQSW) is a Visiting Professor of Social Work at the University of Bedfordshire. She works as an independent foster carer reviewing officer and currently chairs three local authority fostering and adoption panels. She worked as a social worker and a social work manager in inner London before moving into social work education. Her publications focus on social work with lesbians and gay men and fostering and adoption.

1

Introduction

This guide builds on best practice for conducting foster carer reviews.

In recent years, the United Kingdom's (UK) four nation governments have tried to improve the experiences of and life chances for foster children. A key mechanism for improving the quality of foster care is through foster carer reviews. They are conducted in order to evaluate a foster carer's practice and offer the opportunity for improving the quality of foster care. Since the publication of the first edition of this Good Practice Guide, BAAF published a further guide to collecting and analysing information for foster carer reviews (Adams, 2014), advising on best practice when using the BAAF Form FR (England). This publication and the Adams publication can be helpfully considered together.

Foster carer reviews are governed by regulation and require an assessment of whether or not a foster carer and their household remain suitable to care for foster children and if their terms of approval are still appropriate. They provide a formal arena to consider: the quality of each foster carer's care of individual foster children; how the foster carer's development can be enhanced to enable them to improve their practice; and how a fostering service provider (FSP) can support them to undertake their complex work. The foster carer review is a symbolic and practical representation of the relationship between the foster carer and their FSP. It acts as a vehicle for improving an individual foster carer's support, supervision and practice.

Improving the quality and stability of foster care is of paramount importance given that the majority of looked after children in the UK live with foster carers. In England on 31 March 2014 there were 51,340 children placed with foster carers, 75 per cent of the total looked after children population. On 31 July 2014 in Scotland that number was 5,533, 36 per cent of the looked after children population. In Wales it was 4,407, 77 per cent of the looked after children population, and in Northern Ireland it was 2,156, 75 per cent of the looked after children population (BAAF, 2015). Given the high percentage of looked after children who are placed with foster carers across the UK, ensuring that foster carers' practice is as good as it can be and that foster carer reviews are effective is critical.

STRUCTURE

Chapters 2–4 set out knowledge informing good practice. Chapters 5–8 cover the detail of the review process itself. The first substantive chapter (Chapter 2) outlines the current legal and policy frameworks for foster carer reviews within the four nations of the UK. Understanding the legal mandate for foster carer reviews is fundamental to good practice and I therefore cover this at the start of the guide. Chapter 3 considers recommendations and findings arising from inquiry reports and serious case reviews involving foster carers. These reports are important because they remind us of the serious nature of the professional judgements involved regarding whether a foster carer continues to be a suitable person to care for looked after children as well as enabling learning from the case studies that each inquiry represents. Chapter 4 looks at social work knowledge underpinning assessment and review processes. Chapter 5 moves on to look at the practicalities involved in foster carer reviews and addresses necessary administration enabling reviews to be effective and undertaken within the regulatory timeframes and requirements. Chapter 6 covers information gathering for foster carer reviews including who might be approached to provide evidence about the quality of a foster carer's work.

In consulting with people across the UK when preparing this guide, it became apparent that not all FSPs undertake an annual review meeting with the foster carer and their supervising social worker (SSW), where the paperwork prepared for the review is properly scrutinised, separate from the fostering panel process. I argue in this guide that good practice dictates that a review meeting should be held for every foster carer review. Chapter 7 addresses the review meeting's purpose, content and process. Chapter 8 discusses foster carer reviews and their relationship to fostering panels.

EXPLANATIONS

This guide is written for all the nations of the UK. Chapter 2 outlines the legal, policy and regulatory frameworks for each of them. Fostering regulations, guidance and standards are regularly in a state of flux so this guide tries to grasp essential best practice irrespective of the current state of fostering guidance and regulation. When I refer to standards and regulations, other than in Chapter 2, I am referring to those of England, for ease of reading. As stated elsewhere, this guide focuses on good practice within a legislative framework but not on the legislation itself.

Throughout the guide I have used the term fostering service provider (FSP) to cover both local authority fostering services as well as independent fostering providers (IFPs).

I refer to the review administrator in the guide. However, some FSPs do not have a designated administrator for foster carer reviews. Where there is not a review administrator, the tasks will need to be covered by other staff members of the FSP.

Different terms are used for people employed by a FSP who supervise foster carers; they are usually referred to as SSWs in the UK. In this guide I just use the term "SSW" to denote the role of the foster carer supervising social worker.

In the guide the term "reviewing officer" (RO) is used for the person who chairs the foster carer review meeting. I use "RO" whether or not that person is employed by the FSP or is independent. "Independent reviewing officer" (IRO) is used here for the person who chairs a foster child's looked after children's review.

I refer to a foster carer's "own children" to mean children who are: born to them; adopted by them; who are subject to a special guardianship order or a child arrangements order. In other words, a foster carer's own children refers to all children for whom a foster carer has responsibility other than the foster child.

Throughout I refer to a "foster child" and a "foster carer" in the singular. When I use the term foster child, I am, by the use of that term, including fostered young people.

When I refer to "foster care", I am encompassing all types of foster care in its varied forms governed by fostering regulations, including family and friends foster care.

SUMMARY

There is surprisingly little published about foster carer reviews other than that which is within regulations, standards, guidance and codes of practice (Adams, 2014; Brown, 2014a, 2014b). Mehmet is one of the few people who has written about foster carer reviews in her book about the UK National Standards for Foster Care (UKNSFC) (UK Joint Working Party on Foster Care, 1999a) and the then Fostering Services National Minimum Standards (DH, 2002) (Mehmet, 2005). Like Mehmet, this guide draws on the UKNSFC which have weathered the sands of time and although dated and not legally binding, still have helpful things to say about good practice for foster carer reviews.

I am mindful when writing this guide of the excellent social work and foster care practice there is across the UK. In writing a good practice guide the author inevitably can sound a little pompous and over directive. In preparing this guide I have remained respectful of the experience and excellent practice that there is and hope I do not seem as if I am teaching grandmothers/grandfathers to suck eggs. However, there is currently some variation between FSPs regarding foster carer reviews in how they are undertaken and the degree of rigour expended. This guide is therefore one contribution towards trying to establish what we might mean when we talk about foster carer review best practice.

The current legal and policy framework

INTRODUCTION

This chapter sets out the UK's four nations' current legal and policy framework for foster carer reviews. This legal landscape is an ever-changing terrain and as a result the guide can only reflect the legal framework as it was in 2015. I note primary and secondary legislation and some policy documents relevant to foster carer reviews but do not cover the specific detail as the original documents should be consulted.

There are similarities and overlaps between the four nations' legal and policy frameworks pertaining to foster carer reviews as well as there being a few significant differences. The chapter starts by considering the UKNSFC (UK Joint Working Party on Foster Care, 1999a) and the related Code of Practice on the recruitment, assessment, approval, training, management and support of foster carers (UK Joint Working Party on Foster Care, 1999b). Both these documents apply to the UK as a whole and are not legally binding. However, although now dated, they still offer direction regarding best practice in foster care. Northern Ireland, Wales and Scotland subsequently published their own Codes of Practice. I then address the four nations' legal and policy frameworks in turn.

Laws, regulations and guidance provide a framework for what must be, as well as what can be done. Regulation cannot by itself safeguard foster children's interests. As Brammer writes:

> Policies, legislation, structures and procedures are, of course, of immense importance, but they serve only as a means of securing better life opportunities for each young person. It is the robust and consistent implementation of these policies and procedures which keeps children and young people safe.

> (Brammer, 2010, p166)

In other words, it is the quality of the implementation of laws, policies and regulations that makes a difference to young people and children.

In the UK, legislation about the welfare of children and young people focuses on the best interests of the child. This is stated in primary legislation in England, Wales, Scotland and Northern Ireland. The Children (Northern Ireland) Order 1995, the Children Act (Scotland) 1995, the Children Act 1989 and the Children Act 2004 all state that children's welfare has to be the paramount consideration. This also has to be the case for foster carer reviews. The welfare of a specific foster child, or a hypothetical foster child who might be placed with a foster carer in the future, has to be the primary focus.

THE UK NATIONAL STANDARDS FOR FOSTER CARE AND THE CODE OF PRACTICE

The *UK National Standards for Foster Care* (UKNSFC) and the *Code of Practice on the Recruitment, Assessment, Approval, Training, Management and Support of Foster Carers* apply to all four UK nations (UK Joint Working Party on Foster Care, 1999a, 1999b). They were the first attempt to create a code of practice and national standards for foster care. Mehmet, writing about the UK National Standards and Code of Practice, says:

> *These two documents set out to establish what was to be expected from everyone involved in foster care, the fostering teams, children's social workers and carers. The work of the Joint Working Party on Foster Care which produced these documents opened the way for standards in foster care to be recognised across the United Kingdom.*

(Mehmet, 2005, p3)

The English, Scottish and Welsh Governments subsequently published their own national standards for foster care. Wales, Scotland and Northern Ireland have all developed their own Code of Practice.

Although the UKNSFC and Code of Practice were not legally binding, they did in effect establish best practice guidance in foster care. They remain helpful detailed documents about foster carer reviews. Standard 16 and its 11 sub-sections address the annual review of foster carers. Standard 16 emphasises the importance of both reviewing individual foster carers and strategic planning being informed by the review process.

As stated earlier, the UKNSFC are not legally binding but rather offer direction regarding best practice. With the Fostering Network's permission, I have reproduced Standard 16 of the UKNSFC in full:

16. Annual reviews with carers

A joint review is conducted with each carer at least once a year in a manner that satisfies the authority of the continuing capacity of the carer to carry out the fostering task, provides the carer with an opportunity to give feedback, contributes to essential information on the quality and range of service provided by the authority, and informs recruitment, assessment and training strategies.

There is an agreed format for the review which incorporates both the assessed performance of the carer and the carer's assessment of the quality of service and support provided by the authority, as well as any required updates of statutory checks.

A review report is compiled by the supervising social worker, incorporating the written views of each social worker responsible for any child placed in the foster home since the last review, the views of children who are fostered and their parents where appropriate, and the views of the carer, her or his sons and daughters and any other household members.

The review report includes an action plan for the next twelve months, identified training and support needs of the carer and a recommendation regarding continued approval of the carer, and the numbers and ages of children for whom she or he is approved.

The carer has the opportunity to read the review report and to contribute her or his own written comments.

The review includes repeats of all statutory checks and references for the carer at least once every three years.

A review meeting is held that includes the carer and the supervising social worker, and is chaired by an appropriate third party, who can form an independent judgement and is knowledgeable about foster care.

Where necessary, the carer is supported to play a full part in the review through provision of disabled access, translation and interpreting facilities.

Each annual review of a carer requires the endorsement of the fostering panel; where there is any change in the circumstances of the carer, or the outcome of the review is a recommendation for change or termination of approval, a recommendation or decision is reached by the panel and the carer has the right to put her or his view to the panel meeting.

The carer receives written notification of the outcome of the review and the reasons for it, together with details of any appeal or complaints procedure.

The report of the review meeting and its outcome are recorded on the carer's file, together with any relevant comments or objections from the carer.

An additional review is held following any significant incidents, complaints or allegations of abuse or neglect.

(UK Joint Working Party on Foster Care, 1999a, p46)

The UKNSFC and the related Code of Practice give best practice direction for foster carer reviews and, where best practice is the aim, they should be adhered to in addition to the legal and policy frameworks for each of the four nations.

NORTHERN IRELAND

The Children (Northern Ireland) Order 1995 is the central piece of legislation in Northern Ireland concerned with child welfare. Like the Children Act 1989, the Children Act 2004 and the Children Act (Scotland) 1995, it states that the welfare of a child is paramount. There are six volumes of related guidance and regulation with the most pertinent to foster carer reviews being Volume 3.

The Children (Northern Ireland) Order 1995 Guidance and Regulations Volume 3 Family Placements and Private Fostering

The guidance sets out the statutory framework for foster care. Chapter 4 sections 42–49 give detailed direction regarding foster carer reviews (Department of Health and Social Services and the Office of Law Reform, 1995). The guidance complements and provides the detail to the regulations covered below.

The Foster Placement (Children) Regulations (Northern Ireland) 1996

Regulation 4 (1)–(6) sets out the framework for foster carer reviews. It states the timeframe for reviews (minimum annually), who should be consulted, and covers the relationship between the review process and the fostering panel. It also states the procedure for terminating a foster carer's approval. The purpose of the review is noted as being to ascertain whether or not a foster carer and their household continue to be suitable to care for foster children (Department of Health and Social Services and the Office of Law Reform, 1996, section 4 (1)).

Code of Practice on the Recruitment, Assessment, Approval, Training, Management and Support of Foster Carers

The Northern Ireland Department of Health and Social Services published their own Code of Practice in 1999 (Department of Health and Social Services, 1999). Sections 4.21 and 4.22 cover foster carer reviews. This Code of Practice should be consulted by those undertaking foster carer reviews and complements the 1996 Foster Placement Regulations and Volume 3 of the Northern Ireland Order 1995 Guidance and Regulations.

Care Matters in Northern Ireland – A Bridge to a Better Future

Care Matters in Northern Ireland: A bridge to a better future was published in 2007. As well as addressing family support and child protection, it covers the quality and stability of foster placements (Department of Health, Social Services and Public Safety, 2007). Although it does not address foster carer reviews directly, its content is important in terms of trying to improve the quality of foster children's lives and should be noted by those undertaking foster carer reviews.

To date, Northern Ireland does not have its own national standards for foster care. In 2009, the Fostering Network expressed its concern regarding this and Kate Lewis, the Director of the Fostering Network Northern Ireland, said:

> *Fostered children have the same rights and needs wherever they live. But while those in England, Scotland and Wales are currently assured of minimum standards of service and care, children who live in Northern Ireland are not. This is just not right. As a matter of urgency we need to see minimum standards for foster care introduced so that all fostering services come under the same levels of scrutiny. This should go some way to ensuring that all fostered children are treated equally, and are properly looked after by their fostering service and foster carers.*

(The Fostering Network, 2009)

At the time of writing, Northern Ireland still had no national standards for foster care other than the UKNSFC (UK Joint Working Party on Foster Care, 1999a).

WALES

The Children Act 1989, Part 3 of the Children Act 2004 and the Children Act 2004 (Commencement No. 8) (Wales) Order 2008 provide the legal framework for the welfare of children in Wales.

Code of Practice, Wales: Recruitment, Assessment, Approval, Training, Management and Support of Foster Carers

In 1999, Wales, like Northern Ireland and Scotland, published its own Code of Practice, which includes foster carer reviews (Wales Code of Practice Working Group, 1999). This Code of Practice should be noted by those undertaking foster carer reviews alongside the National Minimum Standards for Fostering Services and the Fostering Services (Wales) regulations.

National Minimum Standards for Fostering Services (NMSFS)

The Welsh Assembly published their NMSFS in 2003. These NMSFS set the standards that are expected for FSPs in relation to their roles and responsibilities pertaining to the care of foster children (Welsh Assembly Government, 2003). Although foster carer reviews are mentioned in this document, there is little detail.

The Fostering Services (Wales) Regulations 2003

Regulation 29 (1)–(12) covers foster carer reviews and sets: timeframes for reviews (minimum annually); who should be consulted, the relationship between the review process and the fostering panel, and regulations regarding a foster carer's continuing approval, their terms of approval and changes to their terms of approval or the termination of their approval.

The primary purpose of the review is to establish if the foster carer continues to be suitable to act as a foster carer and that their household continues to be suitable and that their terms of approval continue to be appropriate (The National Assembly for Wales, 2003).

Children and Young People: Rights to Action

Children and Young People: Rights to Action sets out the framework for the welfare of children in Wales (Welsh Assembly Government, 2004). It does not address foster carer reviews but is a document with which those who are working with foster carers and undertaking foster carer reviews should be familiar.

SCOTLAND

The Children (Scotland) Act 1995 is the primary piece of legislation that covers the welfare of children in Scotland.

Code of Practice on the Recruitment, Assessment, Approval, Training, Management and Support of Foster Carers in Scotland

The Code of Practice was published by the Scottish Executive and the Fostering Network in 2004. Like the UK equivalent (UK Joint Working Party on Foster Care, 1999b) it has a specific code (4.9) addressing foster carer reviews. The detail of this code is now out of date as it refers to the Fostering of Children (Scotland) Regulations 1996 which have been superseded by the Looked After Children (Scotland) Regulations 2009. However, it still has relevant and useful content (The Scottish Executive and The Fostering Network, 2004).

National Care Standards Foster Care and Family Placement Services

The national standards published in 2003 were revised in 2005 and set the standards expected for foster care in Scotland. Standard 11 addresses foster carer reviews and is worded in such a way as to address foster carers directly. Standard 11.1 states that foster carer reviews will be held annually (The Scottish Executive, 2005a).

The Looked After Children (Scotland) Regulations

These regulations, published in 2009, include regulations 25 and 26 governing foster carer reviews. They set the timeframes which dictate that reviews of newly approved foster carers should take place within 12 months of their approval and thereafter within three years of the previous review. This three year requirement contradicts the National Care Standards (The Scottish Executive, 2005a) requirement for annual reviews. Best practice would dictate that foster carer reviews, as a minimum, should be held annually. This contradiction is picked up in the Guidance on the Looked After Children (Scotland) Regulations (The Scottish Government, BAAF and the Fostering Network, 2010).

The regulations state that foster carer reviews should consider the foster carer's suitability to continue caring for foster children, the development of the foster carer and their terms of approval. The regulations note: who should be consulted, the relationship between the review and the fostering panel, and the procedures for continuing a foster carer's approval, changing their terms of approval or terminating their approval (The Scottish Executive, 2009).

Guidance on Looked After Children (Scotland) Regulations 2009 and the Adoption and Children (Scotland) Act 2007

Published in 2010, this guidance complements the 2009 regulations offering detailed consideration of foster carer reviews. The guidance provides full, detailed and helpful direction on how foster carer reviews should be conducted. It notes that although the Looked After Children (Scotland) Regulations stipulate that foster carers have to be reviewed only every three years after their first review, one can be called at any time if the FSP thinks it is necessary or appropriate to safeguard the welfare of any child (The Scottish Government, BAAF and the Fostering Network, 2010).

Getting it Right for Every Child – Proposals for Action

GIRFEC or "getting it right" established a national framework for working with children and young people in Scotland. It is similar in some respects to England's *Every Child Matters* initiative (DfES, 2004). It does not explicitly address foster carer reviews but its "indicators of well-being" for children should be taken into account when evaluating a foster carer's direct care of foster children. There are eight indicators of well-being: healthy; achieving; nurtured; active; respected; responsible; included and safe. The hope is that these indicators of well-being, if in place, will enable children and young people to become: successful learners; effective contributors; confident individuals and responsible citizens (The Scottish Executive, 2005b).

ENGLAND

The Children Act 1989 and the Children Act 2004 are the two main pieces of legislation concerned with the welfare of children. The paramountcy of a child's welfare is stated in both.

The Fostering Services: National Minimum Standards

The Department for Education (DfE) published the *Fostering Services: National Minimum Standards* (NMS) in 2011 under section 23 of the Care Standards Act 2000. This sets out the expectations for the standards that must be met by fostering services. The 2011 NMS have little to say of any detail about foster carer reviews (DfE, 2011a); unlike the UKNSFC (UK Joint Working Party on Foster Care, 1999a). Standard 13.8 states:

> *Reviews of foster carers' approval are sufficiently thorough to allow the fostering service to properly satisfy itself about their carers' ongoing suitability to foster.*

(DfE, 2011a, p29)

Fostering Services (England) Regulations 2011

These regulations were published by the DfE in 2011 (DfE, 2011b) and regulation 28 covers foster carer reviews. This includes: timeframes (minimum annually); who should be consulted; the relationship between the review process and the fostering panel; and regulations regarding foster carers' continuing approval, their terms of approval, changes to their terms of approval and the termination of their approval. The purpose of the review is stated as being to consider whether the foster carer continues to be suitable to foster children, that their household remains suitable and that their terms of approval are still appropriate. The regulations state that in undertaking the review the FSP must seek and take account of the views of the foster carer, any child placed with that foster carer and any authority that has placed a foster child since the foster carer's approval or since their last review. The Independent Review Mechanism's (IRM) relationship to the foster carer's review, the fostering panel and the FSP agency decision maker (ADM) is noted.

The Children Act 1989 Guidance and Regulations Volume 4: Fostering Services

The Children Act 1989 Guidance and Regulations (2011) taken with the NMS (DfE, 2011a) and the Fostering Service (England) Regulations (DfE, 2011b) form the regulatory framework for fostering services in England under the Care Standards Act 2000. Sections 5.59–5.63 refer to foster carer reviews and cover similar content to the regulations (DfE, 2011b) including: timescales (annually); who should be consulted; and the relationship between the review process, the fostering panel and the IRM. The purpose of the review is stated as being to consider if the foster carer and their household continue to be suitable to care for foster children.

Every Child Matters: Change for Children (ECM)

HM Government's White Paper *Every Child Matters* (ECM), published by the Department for Education and Skills (DfES) in 2004, established the national framework for children's services that would 'maximise opportunity and minimise risk' (DfES, 2004, p2). ECM established five outcomes for children to be facilitated by those responsible for them. These were: be healthy, stay safe, enjoy and achieve, make a positive contribution and achieve economic well-being. The ECM five outcomes were central to the New Labour Government's programme of change and were part of the Children Act 2004. The children's services inspection framework was structured around these five outcomes which need to be reflected within the content of foster carer reviews. Although the language of the Conservative, Liberal Democrat Coalition

Government from 2010 changed the emphasis on 'outcomes' to 'helping children achieve more', at the time of writing ECM remained policy.

Care Matters: Time for Change

The White Paper, *Care Matters*, published by the Department for Education and Skills in 2007, sought to improve the lots of and futures for children in public care. Central to this agenda was improving the quality and stability of foster care.

> *Foster carers are central to many children and young people's experience of care. It is essential that we value and support them and ensure that they are properly equipped with the necessary range of skills.*

(DfES, 2007, pp8–9)

One initiative related to this was the Children's Workforce Development Council's (CWDC) creation of the *Training, Support and Development Standards for Foster Care.*

Assessment and Approval of Foster Carers: Amendments to the Children Act 1989 Guidance and Regulations

The Amendments (DfE, 2013a) set out the two-stage process for the assessment of prospective foster carers as well as some changes to the IRM; the usual fostering limit; reviews and terminations of approval of foster carers; and the role of the agency decision maker (ADM).

A social worker's assessment of a foster carer's capacity to care for particular categories of children at the approval stage, and re-assessment of the appropriateness of a foster carer's terms of approval as part of the foster carer review process, is particularly important, and should be carefully considered at each review (Brown, 2014a).

Training, Support and Development Standards for Foster Care (TSDS)

The Department for Education published guidance in 2012 about the TSDS for "general" foster carers (DfE, 2012a), family and friends foster carers (DfE, 2012b), short break foster carers (DfE, 2012c), and for support foster carers (DfE, 2012d). These Standards complement the NMS (DfE, 2011a) but are specific to training, support and development of foster carers. There are seven Standards which foster carers have to meet within the first year of their approval.

The Children Act 1989 Guidance and Regulations Volume 2: Care Planning, Placement and Case Review 2010

HM Government's guidance and regulations were published by the Department for Children, Schools and Families (DCSF) in 2010. They are part of the implementation of the *Care Matters* White Paper and the Children and Young Persons Act 2008. Volume 2 provides guidance and regulations regarding care planning, case review and the placement of looked after children. They do not specifically address foster carer reviews but practitioners involved with the foster carer review process need to be familiar with the guidance and regulations as they establish the framework for planning for and the care of looked after children. The guidance makes an important point which is relevant to the foster carer review process:

> *Foster carer assessments are designed to identify the ages, number or needs of the children to whom the foster carer is most likely to offer the best care. Research evidence consistently shows that placements outside the terms of approval are significantly more likely to result in placement breakdown, often if there is a foster child already in the household. Where the responsible authority wishes to amend the terms of approval to enable the child to remain with the carer, careful consideration must be made by the fostering panel to ensure that the carer has the capacity to meet the child's needs in the context of the needs of other children in the household.*

(DCSF, 2010, p57)

Delegation of Authority: Amendments to the Children Act 1989 Guidance and Regulations, Volume 2: Care Planning, Placement and Case Review

The amendments (DfE, 2013b) helpfully firm up the expectations placed on local authorities and fostering providers, in respect of the delegation of authority from those with parental responsibility to the foster carer, to enable foster children to live as ordinary lives as possible. The amendments note that delegated authority should be clarified in the placement plan for each foster child. It is good practice to review how the foster carer is managing delegated authority as part of their annual review.

SUMMARY

The four UK nations' legal frameworks for foster carer reviews establish the minimum requirements below which practice cannot fall. Although there are similarities between the four nations, there are

16

some differences. The UKNSFC (UK Joint Working Party on Foster Care, 1999a) still offers a best practice framework which, although dated and not legally binding, complements each of the nations' own legislation.

Legal frameworks have to be understood and adhered to but should be treated as the bare minimum and not the aspirational goal of practice. Foster carer review best practice involves abiding by the letter of the law as a minimum but also developing practice that more than meets the basic legal requirements.

As well as abiding by primary and secondary legislation and policy directives, we need to learn from the relevant findings of childcare inquiries to make sure that we take note of their recommendations to improve social work and foster care practice.

3

Recommendations arising from inquiry reports and serious case reviews

INTRODUCTION

Chapter 2 examined the four nations of the UK's legal, policy and regulatory frameworks for foster carer reviews. Social work and foster care practice has to conform to these legal and regulatory frameworks. In addition, findings and recommendations arising from inquiry reports and serious case reviews, when they have something to say about foster care and in particular foster carer reviews, should be noted. The Department of Health, analysing child abuse inquiries of the 1980s, commented that:

> The single lesson to be learned is that child abuse takes place in foster homes, and this knowledge should affect the manner of selection, the speed of placement, and the social work contact in placement.

> (DH, 1991, p97)

Utting addressed the complexity of this area of social work practice when he wrote:

> Investigations into allegations of abuse in foster care or residential settings differ significantly from investigations into allegations against parents or others in the child's own home. Social workers find themselves examining the actions of people regarded as co-workers or professional colleagues.

> (1997, p182)

Deaths and serious abuse of children in foster homes is not the norm; indeed it is rare. However, some inquiry reports and serious case reviews are testament to the fact that sometimes things do go seriously wrong in foster care. Most importantly these reports remind practitioners and FSPs of the need to be rigorous in the assessment, supervision and review of foster carers.

Reder and Duncan, writing about inquiry reports relating to child deaths, not just those related to foster care, wrote:

The consistency between the findings is striking, with particular clusters around: deficiencies in the assessment process; problems with inter-professional communication; inadequate resources; and poor skills acquisition or application.

(Reder and Duncan, 2004, p96)

These "clusters" are similarly borne out in the inquiry reports and serious case reviews involving foster carers, as identified in this chapter.

There have been a number of inquiry reports and serious case reviews since 1945 where either a child has died whilst in foster care or where they have been seriously abused. The reports have examined what went wrong in each of these cases as well as making recommendations for the future in the hope of decreasing the likelihood of similar circumstances recurring. If we are to develop good practice in foster care, it is important that we are aware of these findings and recommendations.

The inquiry report looking at foster carer reviews in most depth is the Wakefield inquiry report (Parrott *et al*, 2007). There are a number of other reports that, although not addressing foster carer reviews directly, cover salient areas. For the purposes of this guide, I have selected the following to consider: the Dennis O'Neill inquiry (Home Office, 1945); the Shirley Woodcock inquiry (Hammersmith and Fulham, 1984); the Derbyshire and Nottinghamshire inquiry (Derbyshire and Nottinghamshire, 1991); the Wakefield inquiry (Parrott *et al*, 2007); the Serious Case Review of Mrs Spry (Gloucestershire Safeguarding Children Board, 2008); the Serious Case Review of Child V and Mr and Mrs A (Rotherham Safeguarding Children Board, 2009) and the overview report on Mr and Mrs B (Rotherham Safeguarding Children Board, 2010). This is by no means an exhaustive list. Brandon *et al*'s analysis of 2005–2007 serious case reviews found that, of the 189 cases they analysed, seven (4%) of the children at the time of the incident were living in foster care (Brandon *et al*, 2009, p27). Not all of these incidents were perpetrated by a foster carer. Unfortunately the report gives too little detail about these seven cases for there to be emerging messages relevant to this guide.

I have not covered reports that considered the deaths of children placed with prospective adopters as this guide's focus is on foster care and foster carer reviews.

INQUIRY REPORTS AND SERIOUS CASE REVIEWS 1945–2010

It is beyond the remit of this guide to go into the detail of the circumstances and recommendations of each case; rather I have selected relevant material related to, but not necessarily about, foster carer reviews. I look at each report in chronological order and then draw together, from the findings of all seven reports, matters relevant to foster carer reviews.

Dennis O'Neill

Dennis (12) and his brothers Terrance (9) and Fredrick (7) were in the care of Monmouth County Council. Dennis and Terrance were placed with Mr and Mrs Gough of Bank Farm, Minsterley in Shropshire. Dennis was placed with the Goughs on 28 June 1944 and Terrance joined him on 5 July 1944. Dennis died on 9 January 1945. Reginald Gough was subsequently found guilty of manslaughter and received a six-year prison sentence and Esther Gough was found guilty of neglect and received a six-month prison sentence. The inquiry report recounted the serious injuries found on Dennis and the degree of neglect and under nourishment he had experienced (Home Office, 1945). Dennis had been placed with the Goughs for just over six months.

The report commented on the acute shortage of foster carers and county council staff to undertake supervision of placements at the time Dennis and Terrance were placed at Bank Farm. It noted that the Goughs had not been thoroughly assessed or references properly sought and that all the rooms of the house had not been considered as to their suitability for fostering.

The report identified inadequate communication between the two councils involved regarding who was responsible for the supervision of the foster home and the children. There was wrangling over levels of remuneration for the foster carers; Monmouth paying a higher rate and Shropshire fearing that other Shropshire foster carers would become disgruntled if they became aware that the Goughs were on a higher rate of payment. The then Boarding Out Regulations related to the 1933 Children and Young Persons Act requirements for visits to children boarded out with foster carers were not met; indeed no visits took place between 28 June and 10 December 1944. At one point both councils had children placed with the Goughs but neither was aware that that was the case. When they did eventually realise, the Shropshire children (the Mullinders) were moved to other foster carers in October 1944. The two Shropshire council staff who originally placed the Mullinder siblings with the Goughs on 12 July 1944 reported that they thought the Goughs' farm house was 'very bare, comfortless and isolated' (Home Office, 1945, p11). However, the Shropshire council member of staff who had undertaken the assessment of the Goughs was of a different view and declared herself to be 'definitely satisfied with the house' (Home Office, 1945, p11).

Dennis and Terrance went to a school in Hope where their attendance tailed off in November and December 1944. Neither child was seen by a doctor during their placement. When eventually a Newport council officer (Mrs Edwards) visited the children on 20 December 1944, she realised that the placement was not satisfactory and described Dennis as looking 'ill and frightened' (Home Office, 1945, p14). She 'saw little affection on the part of the Goughs for the children' (Home Office, 1945, p14). She asked Mrs Gough to take Dennis that day to a doctor. She did not interview the children separately from the Goughs, neither did she ask to look around the house or see the children's bedroom. The same day she recommended that the children should be immediately removed. However, for a number of reasons, including serious flaws in communication between and within the two councils, the children were not removed and Dennis died on 9 January 1945, having not seen a doctor after Mrs Edwards' visit of 20 December 1944.

Sir Monkton, the report's author, concluded that the 1933 Children and Young Persons Act and the Rules for Boarding out Poor Law Children were adequate but the practice and administration in the case were not. He wrote:

> What is required is rather that the administrative machinery should be improved and informed by a more anxious and responsible spirit... The boarding-out rules ought plainly to be obeyed in the letter and the spirit. Their requirement should be treated as a minimum, not a barely attainable maximum.

(Home Office, 1944, p18)

Despite Sir Monkton's conclusion that the legislation and regulations did not, in his view, contribute to Dennis O'Neill's death, his report was one of the contributory factors leading to the setting up of the Curtis Committee (Curtis, 1946), which laid the ground for the Children Act 1948 and the 1947 Home Office and Ministry of Health regulations on the boarding-out of children (Corby *et al*, 2001). This marked the start of the pattern of tinkering with the legislative and procedural frameworks in response to child deaths.

Shirley Woodcock

Shirley died on 4 April 1982, aged 3 years and 3 months, whilst placed with foster carers. Shirley and her brother (4) were placed with their foster carers on 10 December 1981. Both children had considerable emotional needs which, the report concluded, were more than their foster mother could manage. The report identified areas pertinent to this guide as follows: some of the social workers' visits to the family were not recorded; there was fundamental disagreement between the fostering team and the team responsible for the child, the former thinking that Shirley and her brother should be moved from the placement and the latter that a further move would be too disruptive for them; the foster mother described Shirley as being a "faddy eater" whereas the same child had recently been described as having a good appetite; marks and scratches were noticed on Shirley by a fostering officer on 28 January 1982 on a home visit and at that time Shirley was wetting herself, soiling, and had sleep problems; on 16 March a child minding visitor noticed a row of bruises around Shirley's neck which the foster mother explained as being self-inflicted; a health visitor who saw Shirley on 19 March 1982 noted that there were problems in the placement. Around this time Shirley's nursery also reported bruising.

Shirley was admitted to hospital on 4 April 1982 with a head injury (ostensibly related to having fallen out of a cot onto her head) and 50 bruises on her body. Her brother, when examined, also had extensive bruising. Shirley was in this placement for just over four months and was not seen by a social worker for a two-month period during that time.

Shirley's foster mother complained of headaches while the children were placed with the foster family, and visited her doctor on four separate occasions. Reder *et al* note the importance of this sort of information.

> *Some parents gave hints in a disguised way that abuse was escalating, so that the practitioner first needed to translate the information in order to become aware of its significance...In the weeks preceding Shirley Woodcock's death, her foster mother repeatedly told the childminder and general practitioner about her severe headaches.*

(1993, p91)

The report noted that assessments of foster carers only ever give a prognosis regarding their future capacity and abilities to care for children in public care.

> *At the point of approval, new foster parents are untried and untested. Thereafter, it must never be taken for granted that simply because they are approved as foster parents, they will always be able to cope.*

(Hammersmith and Fulham, 1984, p37)

The first review of a foster carer and subsequent reviews offer opportunities to evaluate a foster carer's abilities to "cope" and to test out the prognosis reached in the assessment report.

Derbyshire and Nottinghamshire

On 4 December 1989 Janet Jones, a foster carer, received four concurrent prison sentences including a life sentence for the manslaughter and indecent assault of GS, a 9-month-old baby, and the wilful ill-treatment of and grievous bodily harm to SH, a toddler.

Mr and Mrs Jones lived in Nottinghamshire and were approved as foster carers for Derbyshire County Council. Mrs Jones had a history of depression but this did not come to light in her medical report for the fostering panel approval process. SH, a 16-month-old boy, was placed with them from 1 April 1980 to 2 August 1981. In August 1980, SH sustained a burn injury to his hand for which Mrs Jones sought hospital treatment. She later commented to a social worker that SH 'seemed to feel no pain' (Derbyshire and Nottinghamshire, 1991, p14). On 6 January 1981, Mrs Jones telephoned SH's social worker saying that SH needed to go to hospital as he had lacerated his penis. These injuries were so serious that he subsequently needed three operations. The explanation for the injuries was that having just used the potty he caught his penis in a pushchair mechanism. This explanation, like Mrs Jones' explanation for the burn, was accepted without an investigation and no link was made at the time with his previous injury. On 15 January, his social worker told SH's mother that: 'as far as I was concerned I had no complaints about the Joneses and I would not consider moving him' (Derbyshire and Nottinghamshire, 1991, p17).

During SH's time with the Jones family, Benjamin G was placed on 12 March 1981, when he was under two months old. He had a serious congenital heart disease and died a week later on 19 March 1981.

During Benjamin G's short placement, Karen, Mr and Mrs Jones' adolescent daughter, was admitted to an adolescent psychiatric unit on 16 March 1981, returning home on 24 March 1981. During her stay she disclosed to the unit staff that her parents' relationship was poor and that she was afraid to leave her mother alone with SH. She said that she had seen her mother bang SH's head on the floor and force food down his throat. This was relayed by the unit by telephone to the Social Services Department (SSD). This referral was complicated by the unit staff saying that the information was confidential. SH's social worker, having received this information, wrote in the file: 'decided not to remove SH on this information may be inaccurate, fantasy or part of K's illness' (Derbyshire and Nottinghamshire, 1991, p20). No link was made to SH's previous injuries.

In June 1981, a new social worker was allocated to SH's case. In the previous social worker's transfer summary, there was no mention of the burn to SH's hand or the injuries to his penis. On 2 August 1981, SH was returned 'home on trial'. Despite the social worker's seeming failure to identify a worrying pattern of injuries to SH or to follow up the unit's telephone conversation regarding Karen's concerns about her mother's care of SH, the SSD Area Officer did have concerns. A decision was therefore made that no further placements should be made with the Jones family while they had a six-month gap from fostering and work was done with them. Their own daughter's admission to an adolescent psychiatric unit would have been reason alone for this decision to have been made. The inquiry report noted the lack of fostering panel minutes recording the decision-making processes involved with this foster family. The Area Officer was recorded to have thought that Mrs Jones was psychologically ill and that he was worried by SH's accidents. At this point, the Jones' first period as approved foster carers ended.

Mr and Mrs Jones were re-approved by the same council in June 1984. There was no information sought from the adolescent psychiatric unit during this 1984 assessment and no references were taken up. During the re-assessment Mr and Mrs Jones said that all previous family difficulties had been resolved. Commenting on this assessment, the inquiry team noted: 'There were many serious errors and omissions. A contributory cause of them seemed to be a basic disbelief that foster parents could harm a child, coupled with inadequate assessment practices' (Derbyshire and Nottinghamshire, 1991, p45).

The family fostered a number of children short term between July 1984 and 10 April 1988. GS, a baby girl, was placed with the Jones on 29 June 1988. She was just over two months old at the time. The plan was that the placement would last for about three months whilst an assessment was undertaken with her mother to ascertain whether or not she was able to care for GS. If returning to her mother proved impossible, GS would be placed with an adoptive family. GS was described as being passive with food and there were concerns regarding her poor weight gain. On one occasion she was found by the hospital to have a urine infection. During this placement, Mrs Jones cancelled or changed a number of adoption medical appointments for GS as well as GS' medical appointments set up to monitor her weight.

By December 1988, prospective adoptive parents were being considered. They visited the Jones' home on 2 December 1988 and reported that they had found lumps behind GS' ears and that they thought she seemed small. Mrs Jones later reported that she had taken GS to see the GP and that the lumps behind GS' ears were thought by the doctor to be swollen glands. On 5 January 1989, GS' social worker received a call from Mrs Jones to say that they had had a difficult Christmas because of family members having colds and that she did not want to take GS to see the dietician on 6 January as planned. However, Mrs Jones did go to the hospital for the appointment with GS and GS' social worker but said that GS should not have her clothes removed to be weighed because of her cold. Both the social worker and the dietician agreed. They were to be seen at the hospital again on 11 January. On 8 January, a member of the fostering team visited Mrs Jones, who said that she wanted GS moved as she was so tired; indeed she wanted to give up fostering altogether. The social worker said that on that visit she 'noticed GS give Mrs Jones a strange look' (Derbyshire and Nottinghamshire, 1991, p60).

The day before the next hospital appointment to monitor GS' weight, Mrs Jones telephoned GS' social worker to say that the appointment would have to be changed as they were going away. The appointment was changed first to 20 January and then to 25 January. At this point, a hospital doctor intervened saying that this appointment was too far away and that GS should be seen at the hospital on 20 January. It later transpired that Mrs Jones was not away with her husband but rather he had taken time to work at home and be on leave. On 18 January, GS was taken by ambulance to hospital where she died the following day. She had a fracture to the skull from which she died and injuries to her vagina and anus and bruising to her buttocks that were inflicted about 10–14 days earlier. She also had a healed fracture of her right clavicle.

The inquiry report noted that GS was seen either at home or the hospital 17 times between 29 June 1988 and 6 January 1989. The first foster carer review undertaken with the family was in 1985. The report notes that 'where there were feedback forms on placements for the foster parent annual reviews, no adverse comment was made and the Joneses continued to impress as a capable and caring family' (Derbyshire and Nottinghamshire, 1991, p64). The report concluded that the previous concerns from their first period of fostering were not sufficiently held in mind. If they had been, then the pattern of wanting to change medical appointments might have been addressed.

Recommendation 15.6 of the report noted that all injuries to a child in foster parents' homes should be recorded on the foster parents' file. Recommendation 18.59 states that 'Prospective foster parents who apply for approval outside their local authority area should, as a precautionary measure, be asked their reasons for so doing' (Derbyshire and Nottinghamshire, 1991, p107). Points raised by this case are examined later in the chapter.

Wakefield

In 2007, the Wakefield inquiry (Parrott *et al*, 2007) examined the circumstances surrounding two male foster carers', IW and CF, sexual abuse of foster children in their care. They had been approved by Wakefield Council in July 2003 as short-term foster carers but were given prison sentences in June 2006 for the sexual abuse of four boys who had been fostered by them. This inquiry raised a number of areas relevant to this guide but in addition, unlike the others covered in this chapter, explicitly addressed foster carer reviews.

IW and CF fostered 18 children during their relatively short fostering career. Laird notes that they were inexperienced foster carers who had many troubled children placed with them as a result of Wakefield Council's shortage of foster carers.

Many of the children placed with CF and IW had previously been sexually abused and exhibited sexualised and challenging behaviour... Any one of these children would have presented considerable challenges in terms of their care even for the most experienced of foster carers. Yet, during the one-and-a-half year period from July 2003 to January 2005 these newly approved foster carers were to look after 18 different children, each with substantial and complex needs.

(Laird, 2010, pp195–196)

The inquiry report noted that social workers involved with the case:

...[had experienced] anxieties on their part about being or being seen as prejudiced against gay people. The fear of being discriminatory led them to fail to discriminate between the appropriate and the abusive. Discrimination based on prejudice is not acceptable, especially not in social work or any public service. Discrimination founded on a professional judgement on a presenting issue, based on knowledge, assessed evidence and interpretation, is at the heart of good social work practice. These anxieties about discrimination have deep roots, we argue – in social work training, professional identity and organisational cultures...

(Parrott *et al*, 2007, p164)

On the same point, Brown and Cocker comment:

This report was a sharp reminder for social workers that alongside the need to make sure that practice and service delivery should never negatively discriminate against people on the grounds of gender, sexuality, age, race, religion and disability (as indeed is required by law in the UK under the Equality Act 2006), social workers also have a professional duty not to lose sight of the need to analyse and synthesise material to form professional judgments. Discrimination in its correct non prejudicial form is an essential ingredient in this analysis and synthesis in social work practice.

(Brown and Cocker, 2011, pp137–138)

Like the Gloucestershire report regarding Mrs Spry below (Gloucestershire Safeguarding Children Board, 2008), the Wakefield inquiry recorded the power of CF and IW to manipulate the system that was there to supervise, monitor and support them. Related to a particular incident and their supervising social worker's failure to challenge the foster carers, the report noted:

This significant breach of their boundaries as foster carers was not addressed and challenged, once again signalling to CF and IW that they could be successful in bullying and manipulating the system to get what they wanted.

(Parrott *et al*, 2007, p88)

In 2004, the Commission for Social Care Inspection noted that Wakefield Council's annual foster carer reviews 'had not always been undertaken, and where they had, these were not brought back to panel. This is a regulatory failing which needs addressing...' (Parrott *et al*, 2007, p30).

IW and CF's first annual review on 6 July 2004 was deferred halfway through and re-convened on 14 September 2004. The review meeting was halted by the RO because material came to light that he had not had the opportunity to consider. In line with Wakefield Council's own procedures, prior to the review meeting the RO would have expected to have had copies of written contributions from the foster carers, the SSW and the social workers for each of the children placed with IW and CF since their approval as well as their most recent health report. Not all of these documents were made available by the 6 July review meeting.

The inquiry team concluded that the SSW had written the foster carers' contribution for them for the 14 September review and surmised that because the foster carers had not done their review paperwork the SSW covered for this by doing it for them. The inquiry team thought that in part this was related to IW and CF's bullying relationship with their SSW and her resulting inability to challenge them. The report comments on the poor quality of the SSW's paperwork presented to the 14 September review, as follows: there were inaccuracies in the record of children placed with the foster carers since their approval; there was no record of foster children's views about their placements with CF and IW; there was no record of training that the foster carers had attended since their approval and the SSW's report was described as a 'rambling unstructured narrative' (Parrott *et al*, 2007, p90). The review paperwork had not been checked and signed off by the SSW's manager prior to it being sent to the RO. The RO took weeks before his report from the 14 September review meeting was submitted to the fostering team. The inquiry team concluded that 'decision-making and management oversight in relation to this annual review was poor' (Parrott *et al*, 2007, p82).

At the end of the foreshortened 6 July review, the RO recommended that, despite worrying matters outlined in both the report by a foster child's social worker and a birth parent's letter of complaint about the foster carers, CF and IW should continue to be approved as foster carers and have children placed with them. The inquiry team thought that the RO should have recommended to the fostering panel that their approval as foster carers remain in place but that no children be placed with them whilst matters were further investigated before the re-convened September review.

Commenting on the RO's role in the review meeting of 14 September, the report criticises his lack of rigour and effectiveness and reads as follows:

There is no evidence that IRO challenged or queried the statements or lack of key information in FCW2's report, or that he competently undertook the role of the review chair in facilitating analysis and weighing up information before arriving at conclusions.

(Parrott *et al*, 2007, p92)

Recommendation 27 argues that foster carers' first reviews after their approval should be conducted earlier than the statutory minimum of a year.

The experience of this case emphasises strongly the value of early reviews of all newly approved foster carers, much earlier than the current statutory requirement... It is not appropriate that any potentially damaging and abusive foster carers should be without a review for 12 months.

(Parrott *et al*, 2007, p141)

Mrs Spry

Mrs Spry was an adopter, a local authority foster carer and a private foster carer during the twenty years that she cared for other people's children. She started to foster in 1984 but her caring career was abruptly ended in December 2004 when a young person who had recently left her care disclosed serious abuse.

Mrs Spry had originally privately fostered a sibling group of five. She had been a local authority foster carer from 1985–1994. After 1994 she was no longer a local authority foster carer as, by that time, she had secured orders for each of the children placed with her. From 1994 she removed the children from their schools and home educated them. The report noted that between 1990 and 2000 there were concerns raised regarding Mrs Spry's care of the children on 12 separate occasions. 'However, the referrals seem to have been seen in isolation, with no correlation of the referrals or identification of a concerning pattern of care which was emerging' (Gloucestershire Safeguarding Children Board, 2008, p6).

In September 2000, tragically Mrs Spry's 37-year-old birth daughter and one of the five siblings placed with her, then 16, were killed in a car accident. Two of the other children placed with her were also injured, one seriously. The seriously injured young person was at the time 14. She had to have a number of operations as a result of the accident and because of her injuries used a wheelchair until she finally left the placement. The inference in the inquiry report was that she was kept using the wheelchair longer than was necessary.

In December 2004, the two remaining children placed with Mrs Spry were removed after their sister disclosed the abuse she had experienced. The four young people's disclosures included emotional, physical, sexual abuse and neglect. They had been living in 'squalor, with little in the way of comforts' (London Evening Standard, 2007). When Mrs Spry was tried, Bristol Crown Court heard that the children had been subject to a 'horrifying catalogue of cruel and sadistic treatment' (London Evening Standard, 2007).

There are a number of striking features in this case. The report notes that Mrs Spry had been assessed as to her capacity to care for children as a foster carer and again as an adopter. Although some concerns were raised during the adoption assessment, the report notes that:

> Mrs Spry's application to be a foster parent, and then an adoptive parent, eventually went through without any strong challenges or dissention. Concerns were noted about Mrs Spry's abilities as a parent at times, but, on balance, it was felt to be in the children's interest to remain with Mrs Spry and to have legal security of placement with her. The placements outwardly appeared to be satisfactorily meeting the children's needs. There is some suggestion that Mrs Spry's dominant personality was allowed to drive relationships with statutory agencies.

(Gloucestershire Safeguarding Children Board, 2008, p4)

Mrs Spry was a Jehovah's Witness and although the report does not suggest there is a link between her religion and her abuse of the children, it infers that her religion might have clouded professionals' views about Mrs Spry's parenting style as well as her lifestyle. In other words, social workers might have associated some of her behaviour, quite wrongly, with her religion and have felt anxious about challenging her for fear of seeming negatively discriminatory. Similar dynamics were explored in the Wakefield inquiry (Parrott *et al*, 2007). The Gloucestershire report emphasised the importance of professionals not accepting poor parenting whatever the reason. Recommendation 14 states:

> The impact on the lifestyle of children who are cared for by parents or carers, who display eccentric, unusual or rigid styles of parenting, should be thoroughly assessed. Child protection training should emphasise that eccentric or unusual parenting must not be used as a reason to accept or excuse unacceptable levels of childcare.

(Gloucestershire Safeguarding Board, 2008, p9)

Child V and Mr and Mrs A

Child V was placed with Mr and Mrs A from a hospital special care baby unit by Rotherham Metropolitan Council. She had been treated for neonatal abstinence syndrome as a result of her mother's heroin use during pregnancy. On 7 January 2007, Child V died in hospital from a heart attack and multiple organ failure. She was found to have 13 fractured ribs, which were believed to have been broken about four weeks prior to her death and there was evidence of a more recent re-fracture to one rib. Child V also had tears to her top and bottom lip frenuli and extensive nappy rash. These injuries were believed by Rotherham Safeguarding Board to have been inflicted in the foster home. The police carried out an investigation but no charges were brought.

Mr and Mrs A were approved as short-term foster carers in June 2005. The report records that a foster carer review report was submitted to the fostering panel but no review meeting had been conducted with the foster carers. The report notes that the fostering service 'was under strain and struggling to meet its statutory obligations' (Rotherham Safeguarding Children Board, 2009, p5).

There were four concerning matters about these foster carers' care of children during their fostering career between June 2005 and January 2007 in addition to the serious injuries to Child V. The council's inability to see patterns emerging about these carers' fostering practice and direct care of children was evident. Like the Mrs Spry and the Derbyshire and Nottinghamshire cases, each worrying incident was dealt with in isolation. The report comments on some concerns related to their own birth children – their daughter's weight loss and their son's missed medical appointments.

In the 51 days that Child V was with Mr and Mrs A, the SSW visited the foster family on one occasion. This was pertinent as the fostering manager had gone against the fostering panel's recommendation and the agency decision maker's (ADM) decision that another baby should not be placed with them at the time Child V was placed. The report concluded that: 'There had been a lack of critical analysis of the assessment of the foster carers and their care, made worse by the inadequate level of supervision and review' (Rotherham Safeguarding Children Board, 2009, p8). In addition, the report argued that there needed to be more independent scrutiny of foster carers and that the relationship developed between a foster carer and SSW should not inhibit investigations. The safeguarding board recommended that all recommendations for training made from foster carer reviews should include timeframe requirements.

Mr and Mrs B

Mr and Mrs B were foster carers for Rotherham Metropolitan Council. In June 2008, Mr B was sentenced to 12 years imprisonment for sexual offences against three foster children in his and his wife's care. They had been approved as foster carers in June 1998 and had 13 children placed with them between 1998 and 2008. They had three adult children of their own and four grandchildren.

The Safeguarding Children Board uncovered Mr B's history of alcohol misuse, which had been unbeknown to the fostering panel, also evidence of domestic violence which, however, was not verified. At the start of their fostering career, Mr B was the main carer as Mrs B worked. This changed when Mrs B left her job and Mr and Mrs B both became full-time foster carers. They had health problems but were never re-assessed because of this. Mr B had an oppressive parenting style and the Board's report revealed that children in their care were not interviewed separately from their foster carers. Mr B attended training and indeed became a trainer himself.

In respect of their foster carer reviews, the report observed that: 'Although fostering reviews took place, they did not happen annually, as required by regulations, and it is not clear what information was presented to the fostering panel following each review' (Rotherham Safeguarding Children Board, 2010, p3).

LEARNING FROM INQUIRY AND SAFEGUARDING CHILDREN BOARD REPORTS

These seven reports have a number of findings and recommendations that are either directly about foster carer reviews or salient to them. I have grouped these under the headings used in this guide: the regulatory framework; administration of foster carer reviews; information gathering for reviews; the review meeting and fostering panels.

The regulatory framework

In all the above cases there were breaches of regulations. The O'Neill report (Home Office, 1945) stated that regulations have to be followed to the letter but that they should be treated as a minimum not a maximum requirement. The Rotherham Safeguarding Children Board (2010) report records how, 65 years later, regulations were still not being met. The Department of Health, in its review of inquiry reports of the 1980s, noted in respect to fostering that the then regulations: 'prescribe only minimum standards to safeguard a vulnerable group of children, but even these minimum standards were neglected and some in places, seemed unknown' (1991, p97).

Administration of foster carer reviews

Administration of foster carers' reviews is a crucial function of all FSPs. Effective administration is the only way to ensure that reviews are conducted within the correct timeframes and that necessary information and reports are correctly collected and collated. The Wakefield inquiry report noted how the review paperwork did not even record accurately the names and dates of placements of foster children placed with CF and IW since their approval. In addition, there was no proper record kept of the training these foster carers had attended nor had this information been presented in the review paperwork.

Fostering service regulations require foster carer reviews to be held as a minimum annually or 'whenever the fostering provider considers it necessary' (DfE, 2011b, Regulation 28(2)). This requires those responsible for the supervision of foster carers to assess what change of circumstance or event should trigger the need for an additional or early review. The Derbyshire and Nottinghamshire report recounts the events of March 1981 for the Jones family when they experienced the death of their foster child Benjamin G from congenital heart disease and the admission of their daughter Karen to an adolescent psychiatric unit. Both were major events for any family and should have triggered a review to enable all concerned to consider the impact on their fostering. The Department of Health noted the importance of a proactive stance when it wrote that what was required was: '...a more probing intervention than simply support. Intervention must include sensitive but probing discussion of difficult personal topics; there must be explicit review of the foster family whose structure has changed and this review be undertaken as a matter of high priority' (DH, 1991, p96).

Information gathering for reviews

The regulatory framework governing foster carer reviews states the minimum requirement for information gathering for reviews (DfE, 2011b). This includes a report from the SSW, which covers the views of the foster children, the foster carers and the foster children's social workers for children placed with the foster carer since their approval, for first reviews, or from their last review. For best practice these "views" should be represented in separate reports. These reports are essential but insufficient for a thorough review of a foster carer to be achieved. The above inquiry reports highlight the importance of third party evidence in reviewing and evaluating foster carers. The Woodcock report noted concerns from the nursery, the health visitor and the child-minding officer. The O'Neill report highlighted the significance of Dennis and Terrance's diminishing school attendance and although pre-dating current foster care regulations and the requirement for reviews, it highlights the importance of schools' input into foster carer reviews. Concerns voiced about a foster family by third parties should be considered carefully and taken seriously (DH, 1991, p98).

The importance of foster children's voices being heard in the foster carer review process cannot be overstated. Children need the opportunity to give their opinion of their placements either in writing or by being interviewed separately from their foster carers. The Department of

Health noted that 'social workers spent insufficient time with the children, lacking the skills in some cases to listen to them' (DH, 1991, p98). The UK Joint Working Party on Foster Care conducted consultation with foster children and children of foster carers when preparing the UKNSFC (1999a) and the related Code of Practice (1999b). The children who participated in the focus groups and interviews said their top priority was social workers and foster carers' ability to listen to them. In addition, foster families' own children need to have their voices heard to ensure that their welfare is assured and that fostering is not having a negative impact, and also because they are a source of evidence regarding the quality of the foster care, as was demonstrated in the Derbyshire and Nottinghamshire report.

The Wakefield report noted that a parent of a child cared for by CF and IW complained about the carers and her complaint, as it turned out, was significant. Some FSPs do seek foster children's families' feedback for foster carer reviews and where this is possible it should be pursued.

The Woodcock and the Wakefield inquiry reports highlight disagreements between the fostering teams and the teams responsible for the foster children. Foster children's social workers' reports evaluating the quality of a foster carer's care of children are crucial and enable, where relevant, the foster carer review meeting to explicitly address differences of opinion.

The importance of foster carers' responsibilities for the physical care of children placed with them was addressed in the above reports. The Woodcock inquiry showed how the foster mother was even struggling to manage her own son's medical appointments and the Mrs Spry report noted how the physical care and health of the children was compromised by Mrs Spry. Foster carer reviews should have evidence within the foster children's social workers' reports that medical, dental and optician appointments are up to date.

Both the Spry and the O'Neill reports record the children's appalling living conditions. The SSW's report should include their assessment of the foster home as a suitable environment for children in addition to the health and safety report required by regulations. This requires SSWs to be proactive in regularly seeing the whole house. Writing in the context of child protection but still pertinent to this guide, Ferguson writes:

The necessity to walk around rooms and homes to establish the well-being of children has to be taken as a standard of good social work. When the worker does not move either because they do not realise its importance or because their movement is blocked by service users' tactics, this immobilisation places the child at (higher) risk.

(2010, p1111)

The pattern of Shirley Woodcock's foster mother complaining of headaches was a possible indicator of how far she had ceased to cope. The health of the foster carers needs to be recorded in addition to the regulatory requirement for medical checks.

The importance of the quality of reports submitted for foster carer reviews was highlighted in the Wakefield report. The report noted the good quality of one of the children's social worker's reports and the poor quality of the SSW's report. Reports need to be accurate, critically reflective, analytic and logically argued, to be of use.

The review meeting

The review meeting itself is of paramount importance as here all the materials presented are discussed and a holistic overview of a foster carer's strengths, weaknesses and areas for development can be established. The role of the Chair of this meeting is pivotal. Deficits in this role were noted in the Wakefield report. The importance of all relevant matters being explored was highlighted in the above reports so that emerging patterns about the quality of foster care and dynamics that are being set up between different parties can be identified. The lack of this identification was noted in the Spry and the Woodcock reports.

The SSW and foster carer relationship is a complex one, with the SSW holding the monitoring, supervising and supporting role for the foster carer as they do (Brown *et al*, 2014). The review meeting needs to explore the quality of this relationship to make sure that it is an effective working relationship. This effectiveness requires the SSW to be supportive and empathetic but also probing and rigorous. Ferguson writes:

> *The literature and value base of social work privileges partnership practice with families and empowerment. The use of empathy and negotiation skills is essential to good practice but this has to be combined with an investigative requirement and "detective" sensibility that has been present from its late-nineteenth-century inception…*

> (2010, p1114)

The Spry and Wakefield reports identified bullying dynamics emanating from the carers that impacted on both the judgement and practice of the social workers involved.

In Chapter 4 of this guide, the relationship between assessment and review is explored. The Woodcock, Wakefield, Rotherham (2010), Spry, O'Neill and Derbyshire and Nottinghamshire reports all comment on the inadequacy of the original assessment of the foster carers. When this is the case, subsequent foster carer reviews need to identify gaps. In addition, reviews should pick up on themes and patterns that emerged in the assessment report and identify how these have developed. Reviews offer the opportunity to reappraise the dynamics within a foster family.

Foster carer reviews have to consider in detail each of the placements that the foster carer has undertaken. This is the time where the appropriateness of the matching of the foster child's needs with the abilities and attributes of a foster carer can be seen in the actuality of what has happened during the course of a placement. The Woodcock and the Wakefield reports note that the foster carers were caring for children with particular physical and emotional needs that were probably beyond the carers' abilities to meet. The Woodcock report observed that the foster mother's inability to cope manifested in a number of ways that were not identified by the FSP.

The importance of observation has been identified in the above reports. Le Riche and Tanner cover the knowledge and skills of observation as applied to social work practice and their book is valuable for those working in foster care (Le Riche and Tanner, 1998). When Mrs Edwards visited Bank Farm on 20 December 1944, she knew that Dennis O'Neill's placement with the Goughs was not satisfactory. She observed how Dennis looked, his manner and Mrs and Mr Gough's demeanour towards the children. She was not told about these things, she observed them. The Derbyshire and Nottinghamshire report noted that the worker, on her visit to Mrs Jones on 8 January 1989, observed GS giving Mrs Jones 'a strange look'. If this had been further investigated, then GS' circumstances might have been explored.

The RO has the advantage of being one step removed from the SSW, foster child and foster carer and is therefore in a good position to observe the individuals and the dynamics between them in the review meeting.

Fostering panels

The relationship between fostering panels and foster carer reviews was noted within the Wakefield and Rotherham (2009) reports. In the latter, review paperwork went to the fostering panel without a review meeting having been conducted with the foster carers. The Derbyshire and Nottinghamshire report noted the lack of accurate minute taking of decisions made by the fostering panel. Fostering panels in both their regulatory and quality assurance functions need to comment on the proper conduct of reviews.

SUMMARY

This chapter has focused on seven tragic sets of circumstances that led to either deaths or abuse of children in foster care. Although these situations are rarities, the related reports act as case studies to enable better understanding of how and why sometimes things go very wrong. Heywood, writing about the death of Dennis O'Neill, noted the public reaction to the realisation that children are sometimes harmed in foster care: 'The public disquiet was profound. That a child, removed from his own home because of its bad conditions and entrusted for his greater good, to the public care, should yet experience even worse neglect and cruelty leading directly to his death...' was deeply shocking (1965, p142). When children are removed from their own families and placed in foster care, the bare minimum expected is that they are safeguarded from harm. Foster carer reviews are one mechanism to ensure safeguarding.

Because of FSPs' responsibilities to foster children, it is crucial that we learn from reports' findings and recommendations. Writing over 65 years ago, Sir Monkton's words are still as pertinent now as then and serve to remind social work practitioners and FSPs that regulations have to be followed to the letter but must only ever be seen as a minimum requirement not a maximum attainment (Home Office, 1945).

4

Review and assessment: social work knowledge

INTRODUCTION

This chapter explores social work knowledge informing the process of review. Reviewing is intimately connected to assessment, the terms "assessment" and "review" often going hand in hand. However, what is striking when we look at publications about social work assessment and review is that there is a considerable amount written about assessment in general (Coulshed and Orme, 2006; Milner and O'Bryne, 2009; Martin, 2010; Holland, 2010; Parker and Bradley, 2010; Walker and Beckett, 2010), some about assessment in foster care (BAAF, 1998; Chapman, 2009; the Fostering Network, 2010a, 2010b; Beesley, 2015), but very little about the process of review. Where texts do specifically refer to reviews (Parker and Bradley, 2010), there is no mention of foster carer reviews. This means that seeking out knowledge to underpin practice for foster carer reviews necessitates drawing on that related to assessment as the most relevant body. Inevitably this knowledge has to be adapted to fit the review context. Beesley's text looking at assessment of prospective adopters and foster carers has a helpful section on theoretical approaches to assessment and although the focus is assessment, it is just as relevant to reviews (Beesley, 2015, p19).

Publications about social work assessment tend to focus on assessments where there is a perceived or identified problem for a client or where a client is seen as a potential risk to themselves or to others. This is different from assessments involving making professional judgements about a person or peoples' capacity to formally care for others; as is the case for foster carer assessments and reviews. This means that drawing on knowledge about social work assessment to inform the undertaking of foster carer reviews has limitations and that knowledge has to be selected and moulded to be of use. However, there are key areas from the "general" social work assessment knowledge that are relevant to foster carer reviews and these are covered in this chapter.

It is beyond the remit of this guide to look at knowledge underpinning assessment and review in detail. Rather, I have drawn out selected material that I think helpful when thinking about foster carer reviews. I look first at social work assessment and review in general and then how they relate to foster care in particular. I consider process, communication and lastly, material relating specifically to foster carer assessment and review.

SOCIAL WORK ASSESSMENT AND REVIEW

It is generally accepted that assessment cannot be a one off event but has to be an ongoing process throughout any social work intervention and 'requires both good organisational skills and an holistic understanding of the service user, the practitioner and the professional relationship in which they engage' (Wilson *et al*, 2008, p272). Fostering, because of its regulatory framework, has the foster carer review process built into its practice. This offers the opportunity for a formal re-consideration and updating of the original foster carer assessment as well as evidencing the quality of a foster carer's practice since their approval or last review.

Smale *et al*'s exchange model (1993) emphasises the importance of the relationship between the practitioner and the client or carer for enabling effective assessment work. Parker and Bradley write that this exchange model 'sees service users and social workers exchanging ideas, information and ways forward to make a difference and find alternative ways of approaching the situation being considered' (2010, p15). Wilson *et al*, building on the exchange model, note the importance of relationship-based social work to enable effective assessment and review and argue that it requires the following:

- *a shared and transparent understanding of professional involvement – identifies the pertinent sources of information;*

- *a collaborative construction of the concerns – examines and explores the relevant information in a transparent, reflective and cyclical manner;*

- *a mutually determined analysis – assess and develops a transparent understanding;*

- *a collaborative intervention strategy – jointly constructs a plan of action to respond to the difficulties being faced.*

(Wilson *et al*, 2008, p282)

This approach is necessary for useful reviewing of foster carers as it enables clarity, analysis and transparent planning and decision making.

The model of assessment that many social work practitioners are familiar with in the field of children and families work is the *Framework for Assessment of Children in Need and their Families* (DH, 2000). This framework is underpinned by systemic ideas. A systems approach locates the individual within their social context to fully understand them and their circumstances. This also applies to undertaking reviews: to understand and evaluate the foster carer, the fostering family, their network, their care of foster children and their relationships with foster children's familial and professional networks requires the professionals involved to draw on systems theory.

In addition, psychodynamic ideas are pertinent as fostering relies on the foster carer's use of self. The care of foster children can provoke powerful feelings for those involved and psychodynamic ideas can help social workers and foster carers make sense of feelings and dynamics provoked by the work with which they are involved.

Milner and O'Byrne (2009) look at a number of theoretical approaches to assessment, including systemic and psychodynamic ideas, which can be applied just as well to reviews.

PROCESS

Assessment and review are processes rather than one-off events. As Walker and Beckett write:

> it is important to think of assessment as a process rather than a one-off event. There should be a seamless transition from assessment to intervention in a circular process that includes the crucial elements of planning and reviewing. Once completed, the circle begins again at the assessment stage of the process and so on.

(2010, p13)

A popular model that locates both assessment and review as part of a social work intervention process is what is referred to as ASPIRE. This model, although designed for social work intervention with clients rather than foster carers, is still relevant. It is quite simply a mnemonic: AS – assessment, P – planning, I – intervention, RE – review and evaluation (Sutton, 1999). Foster care is one of the few areas of social work practice where reviews are formalised in the way they are and directly related to the original foster carer assessment.

Milner and O'Bryne define a five stage process for assessment which is relevant to reviews:

- *preparing for the task;*

- *collecting data, including perceptions of the service user, the family and other agencies of the problem and any attempted solutions;*

- *applying professional knowledge (practice wisdom as well as theory) to seek analysis, understanding or interpretation of the data;*

- *making judgements about the relationships, needs, risks, standard of care or safety, seriousness of the situation, and people's capacities and potential for coping or for change (is the progress good enough?);*

- *deciding and/or recommending what is to be done, plus how, by whom and when, and how progress will be reviewed.*

(2009, p4)

The review process involves preparation, collection and collation of data, and analysis of that data prior to the review meeting itself as well as within the meeting. Ultimately the synthesis of the review material, making judgements about whether or not someone remains appropriate to be a foster carer, and whether or not their terms of approval are still appropriate is the kernel of foster carer reviews.

COMMUNICATION SKILLS

Effective assessment and review require social workers to deploy a range of skills as well as be theoretically informed. Coulshed and Orme define these CORE skills required as:

- *Communication*

- *Observation*

- *Reflection*

- *Evaluation*

(2006, p25)

These are all pertinent for effective reviews.

Koprowska's book (2010) on communication and interpersonal skills in social work is particularly helpful for those working in fostering because it covers direct work with individuals, families and communication with children. Communication with children, both a foster carer's own children and foster children, is an integral part of the preparation for a foster carer's review. Luckock and Lefevre (2008) and Lefevre's (2010) books about communicating with children are helpful in that they address imaginative and child-focused ways of engaging children.

Milner and O'Byrne note the importance of core skills in assessments and reviews including 'being punctual, reliable, courteous, friendly, honest and open' (2009, p19). The exchange model draws on the work of Egan (2009) in emphasising the importance of interpersonal communication and interviewing skills and how listening is critically important to effective social work practice. Trevithick (2005), drawing on Egan's work, offers a useful exploration of interpersonal communication and interviewing skills that are essential for social work practice and necessary for reviews to be effective.

The skills of observation were noted in Chapter 3 as being essential to social work practice in fostering. Observing a foster carer with a foster child tells more about that foster carer's ability to show warmth than if the foster carer just talks about their ability to care for children with warmth. Trevithick writes that observation helps us 'understand and to formulate hypotheses about what is actually happening and why, and to check out the reliability of our perceptions against those of other people' (2005, pp121–122). However, making use of observation requires the practitioner to be reflective. Holland comments that, when observing, the practitioner needs to retain a 'reflexive awareness of the impact of their own presence and their beliefs, experience, professional status and knowledge on the interaction' (Holland, 2010, p122). The Fostering Network's social worker's guide to foster carer assessments notes that, as part of the assessment process, there should be an observation of the applicant interacting with children (The Fostering Network, 2010b, p9). For foster carer reviews this is a crucial component and should be drawn on by the SSW in their report for the review.

Relationship-based social work, which is fundamental to foster care, necessitates social workers being able to observe and reflect upon their own feelings and actions. They need to be sufficiently self-aware to be cognisant of their subjectivity enabling them to reach a required safe level of objectivity in their work with foster carers and foster children. Fostering is an area of social work practice which retains an expectation that social workers develop in-depth relationships with foster carers. This is a strength of this area of social work practice but also means that social workers need to be clear about their roles and responsibilities as well as professional boundaries so that they focus on the best interests of foster children and do not get drawn into collusive relationships with foster carers.

Foster carers are a diverse group representing most of the cultures, ethnicities and religions to be found in the UK. There are couples, single people of both genders, lesbians, gay men and transgender people who are foster carers. This means that over time most social workers are likely to be working with foster carers who are different from themselves in some way. This requires what Cree and Myers (2008) refer to as cultural competence. In the previous chapter we saw how the Wakefield inquiry uncovered serious misjudgements on the part of social workers which the inquiry team associated with the social workers' desire to be seen as non-discriminatory. That desire has been linked to what is referred to as anti-discriminatory practice (ADP). Fear of being discriminatory has been shown to have serious negative impacts on social workers' professional judgement. Walker and Beckett elaborate on the complexity of this when they write:

> One of the main tasks of a social worker carrying out assessments is to discriminate. Given that it is generally agreed that social work should strive to be anti-discriminatory, this sounds like an odd thing to say, but there is a difference between being discriminatory and being discriminating. Indeed, though both words refer to making distinctions, they are in some way opposites. Being discriminatory means making bad judgements on the basis of irrational prejudice. The adjective "discriminating", however, refers to the ability to make fine judgements based on skill and knowledge.

(2003, p79)

All social workers must avoid negative discrimination (as they are required to by the Equality Act 2010) at the same time as utilising skills, knowledge and professional expertise to make sound judgements. Cultural competence also has its own pitfalls. Cree and Myers warn of the tendency to think that being taught facts about different cultures can automatically lead to cultural competence, whereas it can result in poor practice as the unique individual is lost in a sea of cultural generalisations (2008, p46). They refer to the work of Husain (2006), who suggests that cultural competence requires social workers to have 'cultural knowledge, cultural awareness and cultural sensitivity' (2008, p46). For these to be translated into effective practice, social workers need enough self-awareness to be able to process their reactions to unfamiliarity and difference and not just to react. In addition, social workers have to have an understanding of the specificity of their own experience and culture.

Foster care is an area of social work practice that provokes strong feelings about families, children, relationships and attachment. We all have our own ideas regarding what is best for children and particularly for foster children who have already been removed from their birth families. Because of this, social workers need a sound knowledge base about what children need in order to enable their physical, emotional and educational development and for them to reach their individual potentials. This knowledge enables social workers to work from a professional position rather than relying on their own personal prejudices. This is as relevant at the foster carer review stage as it is for assessments.

FOSTERING ASSESSMENT AND REVIEW

Writing about reviews in children and families work but not specifically about fostering, Parker and Bradley write:

> ...review is seen... as a continuous process that considers what has been achieved from the planning stage and revises or refines accordingly, similar to an action-planning or action-research cycle. This requires social workers to develop a number of skills: planning; negotiating and consultation; information gathering; discussion and analysis; replanning.

(2010, pp123–124)

The relationship between the foster carer's original assessment and their reviews is fundamental. 'Assessment is a process that continues throughout a foster carer's career and the first review in particular should build on the recommendations of the original assessment report' (The Fostering Network, 2010b, p59).

I have noted above that there is little written about social work assessment as it relates to foster care. There is even less written about foster carer reviews. However, some publications about assessment of foster carers do have material that is relevant to reviews as noted below.

Most FSPs currently use Form F (BAAF, 2014) as a template for undertaking foster carer assessments. Some FSPs use the Fostering Network's *Skills to Foster Assessment* (2010a; 2010b), which sets out a structure for undertaking and recording foster carers' assessments. No such templates exist for foster carer reviews. This can be seen as a weakness but also a strength. One of the problems of templates is that they can be used in a reductive and formulaic fashion. Chapman's guide (2014) to undertaking a fostering assessment, using Form F, sets out a range of questions that assessors should use with applicants and questions for themselves when they analyse the data they have gathered. This text is helpful and potentially facilitates thorough assessments taking place. However, Chapman's questions could be misused. The gathering of information through the use of set questions has its limitations as it can prohibit the foster carer's narrative being told and understood in a holistic manner. Questions should be seen as prompts for the assessor to make sure that no stone has been left unturned. Wilson *et al* caution against a questions approach to assessment when they write:

> Traditional assessment models focus on question-and-answer approaches to gathering information. In contrast, a central characteristic of this stage of the assessment process is its collaborative nature. It is important that practitioners can hear the service user's "story" and can use techniques that ensure an holistic understanding of the service user's perspective views has been obtained.

(Wilson *et al*, 2008, p285)

Wilson *et al*'s caution needs to be held in mind when conducting reviews. Here practitioners are again gathering and analysing information about the review period and the detail of the fostering experience during that time. Chapman rightly places emphasis on the analysis of data during assessment; also required when undertaking reviews. 'Having collected the information, the guide places an emphasis on analysis of the information collected, as this is something that is often identified as lacking in assessments presented to fostering panels' (2009, p3).

A BAAF publication published in 1998 remains an important guide to what assessors need to consider during foster carer assessments. Although its focus is assessing for permanence, it is relevant to foster carers' assessments more generally as well as to reviews. It deals with the emotional complexity of caring for other people's children and the attributes required in foster carers and adopters at the assessment stage and which also need to be evident at the review stages of a foster carers' career. They write that children separated from their birth families need families:

- *with attitudes that are open and flexible rather than closed and rigid;*

- *who can face sadness and loss and are not embarrassed or threatened to talk about the feelings involved;*

- *who can put the needs of children first and not feel undermined by important past relationships;*

- *who are able to look honestly at themselves and acknowledge their strengths and limitations;*

- *who do not expect to do it all on their own and can use and welcome help if it is needed.*

(BAAF Assessment Working Party, 1998, p7)

The Fostering Network's assessment guide for applicants notes the personal qualities that foster carers need. These qualities should be evident in each review and not just within the original assessment document. The first of these, although one would think was self-evident, is important to name:

- *Enjoying the company of children and young people.*

- *Good communication skills.*

- *The ability to work as part of a team.*

- *Being flexible and non-judgemental.*

- *Being able to negotiate and compromise.*

- *Being able to understand and empathise, both with children and with their families.*

(The Fostering Network, 2010a, p9)

Assessment of a foster carer only ever offers a prognosis as to how the assessor believes a foster carer will be with foster children once they are approved and have a foster child placed with them. A foster carer's review, on the other hand, enables that prognosis to be tested out against the realities of the foster care provided to specific children. The attributes and qualities listed above need to be evidenced in reviews through the detail of what the foster carer has actually *done*. Getting to this material in a review is unlikely to be realised through just asking direct questions but rather will materialise through the carer telling the story of their fostering experience with specific foster children.

The foster carer review has to address the dynamics between couples and within the fostering family to make sure that the family is still a benevolent, warm, and cohesive environment for a foster child to live within. At the assessment stage couples and families might appear stable and solid. However, placing a foster child can have profound effects on the dynamics between couples and within families. Reviews offer the opportunity to consider what impact fostering has had on the individuals involved and the family as a whole. The BAAF Assessment Working Party noted this for applicants preparing for assessments and their comments are relevant to foster carer reviews: '...when a child joins a new family that family will never be the same again and neither will the child. The child's emotional turmoil can prove something of a catalyst and can evoke a range of feelings and reactions' (1998, p12). This range of feelings and reactions need to be explored through the review process to see if they are manageable for those involved and are not having a negative impact on the carer's ability to foster and the quality of their direct care of foster children.

The motivation of foster carers can change over time and should be reconsidered at the review stage. Before a child is placed with a foster carer, however thorough the assessment has been, they can still hold fantasies about what it will be like to foster and their capacities as a foster carer. Beesley writes: 'When a child is placed, adopters and foster carers must learn to cope with the reality of themselves as imperfect parents at the same time as dealing with the many and often potentially overwhelming pressures of caring for a very needy child' (2015, p75). The realities of fostering can have a profound impact on the emotional and psychological well-being of individuals and this impact should be addressed as part of the review process.

Beesley's (2015) book about assessment of prospective adopters and foster carers, although focusing on assessment rather than reviews and addressing permanence rather than all forms of foster care, is an invaluable contribution to the literature relevant to both assessment and review. As stated earlier, its section on theoretical approaches to assessment is useful for foster carer reviews.

SUMMARY

To undertake useful and capable social work practice when conducting foster carer reviews, practitioners need to have a pertinent knowledge base. However, as we have seen, there is little published about foster carer reviews, never mind their underpinning knowledge. We therefore have to draw on knowledge about assessments, which is the nearest equivalent area of social work practice. But again, most writing about social work assessment is related to working with clients who have particular needs or pose a risk to themselves or others. Foster care is different, requiring the assessment of applicants' potential to care for foster children. So, to inform foster carer reviews we need to draw on related social work assessment knowledge and draw out what is relevant and of use.

The role of review, as part of social work intervention, has been argued above. I have stated the usefulness of systemic and psychodynamic ideas because they provide maps and tools to facilitate the review process, professional judgement and decision making. Other theoretical approaches are relevant to foster care, indeed social learning theory has been shown to be particularly effective when helping foster carers care for troubled children (Brown, 2014a).

For effective reviews to take place, there needs to be the collection of data about the quality of the foster care that has been accomplished. This collection of data is examined further in Chapter 5. The SSW's review report should include their observations of a foster carer's direct care of foster children. Data, however collected, is only useful when analysed and synthesised.

Walker and Beckett comment on the use of intuition to inform decision making. This is a dangerous area but one that in foster care is often significant. Assessors, SSWs and ROs will sometimes comment about 'just knowing something wasn't right'. This feeling needs to be considered seriously as sometimes it can indicate the 'unconscious processing of data' (Walker and Beckett, 2010, p109). However, they also argue that intuition needs to take its place alongside the analysis and synthesis of all the material gathered for assessments and reviews and that it cannot be relied upon on its own.

Lastly, the most important variable for effective foster carer reviews will be the communication skills of those involved in gathering the information for the review and those conducting the review meeting. To enable a thorough, rigorous and facilitative review process, practitioners need to exhibit attributes that in social work really do make a difference. Koprowska, reviewing research findings on effectiveness in the helping professions, writes that practitioners need to:

> *...demonstrate both personal qualities and technical skill in order to be effective...this body of research...highlights that certain human qualities really do make a difference. Warmth, attention, respect and understanding, when coupled with active and skilled interventions, enable people to feel better and manage their lives better.*

(2010, p23)

Reviews are an opportunity to examine what and why things have gone well for foster carers and their foster children as well as what has not gone well and the reasons. Whether a review is covering positive or negative material, the interpersonal skills of the practitioners involved need always to be facilitative.

5

The administrative process

INTRODUCTION

Effective administration of foster carers' reviews is key to them being undertaken in a timely, rigorous and inclusive manner.

There must be robust administrative and quality assurance arrangements for ensuring reviews take place on time and are undertaken appropriately to the circumstances of foster carers and the children placed (and previously placed and likely to be placed).

(Parrott *et al*, 2007, p141)

This chapter considers foster carer review administration. This includes the smooth running of the review process to make sure that, as a basic minimum, fostering regulations' requirements related to foster carer reviews are met and that reviews are as effective and meaningful as they can be, thus enabling considered decision making. FSPs will have their own administrative systems established to make sure that foster carer reviews are conducted effectively.

By establishing organisational and administrative systems, we are in a position to ensure that we make the best of whatever time and resources we have available to us. This involves devising a...administrative system for planning, organising, monitoring and reviewing our work to ensure that we are keeping to agreed programmes, action plans, targets, aims and objectives, and that these are consistent with the expectations of our agency in terms of policy, practice and administrative structures.

(Trevithick, 2005, p137)

Although fostering agencies have their own systems established for effective foster carer reviews, there is still variation nationally, with some agencies not managing to review all their foster carers within the timeframes set by regulation. This chapter looks at key elements of administration that enable effective reviews to be conducted. I have grouped the administrative tasks into three areas. Firstly, the management of timing and process; secondly, the collection and collation of the review paperwork; and thirdly, the relationship of foster carer reviews to fostering panel processes.

TIMING AND PROCESS

In Chapter 3 it was noted that a number of inquiry reports highlighted that in some cases foster carer reviews had not been conducted within the required timeframes set by regulation. For example: 'Although fostering reviews took place, they did not happen annually, as required by regulations, and it is not clear what information was presented to the fostering panel following each review' (Rotherham Safeguarding Children Board, 2010, p3).

Reviews have to be conducted annually and within the first year after a foster carer's approval (DfE, 2011b). As I have argued earlier, and indeed as was recommended by the Wakefield inquiry (Parrott *et al*, 2007), reviewing a newly-approved foster carer much earlier than a year is good practice. Conducting a foster carer's first review within six months after a first placement is made or within a year since approval, whichever is the sooner, is better practice. Some would argue that the first review should take place within three months of a child being placed with a newly-approved foster carer or within a year of approval, whichever is the sooner. The Wakefield inquiry team in their recommendations wrote:

> *The experience of this case emphasises strongly the value of early review of all newly-approved foster carers, much earlier than the current statutory requirement. The impact on carers, as individuals and as partners, of taking on such a role with often vulnerable and challenging children requires intensive support and supervision. It is not appropriate that any potentially damaging and abusive foster carers should be without a review for 12 months.*

(Parrott *et al*, 2007, p141)

For the purposes of this guide I am proposing that FSPs adopt the Wakefield inquiry's recommendation that first reviews of foster carers should take place sooner than the current regulations require and be conducted within six months after a first placement is made with a foster carer or within the year, since approval, whichever is the sooner. The first review is of particular importance as it is when the assessment made by the assessor about a foster carer's potential is tested out against the reality of the foster carer's practice.

The FSP's foster carer review database should be updated regularly after every fostering panel or after the FSP's ADM's decisions have been confirmed in writing. This database should include the date of the foster carer's approval, the name of their SSW and their SSW's manager, the name of the RO, the date of their last review (where applicable) and the date set for their next review. The date for a foster carer's next review should be set at their review meeting for 11 months hence, unless an earlier review is recommended. Booking the forthcoming review 11 months ahead allows for the possibility of unforeseen circumstances that could lead to an unavoidable postponement of the review meeting date. Setting the date 11 months ahead rather than 12 is a way of making sure that reviews are always conducted within the year.

To make sure that reviews happen at the right time requires there to be dedicated administrative support for this process. The foster carer review administrator should alert a foster carer's SSW to the impending foster carer's review a minimum of eight weeks before the review meeting date. This allows enough time for the SSW to gather all the information and reports needed for the review. The administrator at the same time needs to send the SSW the forms that need completing for the review as it is usually the responsibility of the SSW to make sure that all the necessary forms are completed. When the forms are completed, these need to be returned to the review administrator, collated by them and sent a minimum of one week before the review meeting date to the RO chairing the meeting, the foster carer and the SSW.

It is best practice for the RO not to be the line manager of the SSW, to enable some degree of independent appraisal and judgement to be facilitated. The UKNSFC (UK Joint Working Party on Foster Care, 1999a) advised that the 'review meeting is chaired by an appropriate third party, who can form an independent judgement and is knowledgeable about foster care' (1999, p46). Many FSPs use ROs who are independent of the FSP, thus enabling a greater degree of independence. Whether or not the RO is employed by the FSP, they need to be involved by the review administrator in confirming the dates of reviews they will be chairing. This should be done in a timely manner so there is not a rush to find an RO just before a review meeting.

The RO, having chaired the review, should complete their report, which will be incorporated into the review documentation submitted to the FSP and/or the fostering panel. The Wakefield inquiry identified a problem with delays with ROs' reports being completed in a timely manner after the review meeting had been undertaken. RO reports need to be submitted to the SSW, the SSW manager and the review administrator within a suggested maximum time of three weeks after the review meeting has taken place.

COLLECTION AND COLLATION OF THE REVIEW PAPERWORK

The quality of the paperwork gathered prior to a foster carer's review meeting is crucial as the RO is dependent on this documentation to inform their preparation for chairing the review meeting (Adams, 2014). Both the review administrator and the SSW's manager need to check that all contributors' reports are signed and dated. The SSW's report must be quality assured and signed off by their manager before it is sent as part of the review paperwork to the RO.

The completion of reports for a foster carer's review should enable the engagement of the various individuals who can inform the review process. For foster carers and SSWs, the writing of their reports enables informed reflection upon and evaluation of the quality of the foster carer's practice.

Written contributions for the foster carer's review

The fostering regulations set a minimum requirement regarding whose views should be sought when undertaking foster carer reviews. These include the foster carer, any foster child placed with the foster carer, and the social workers responsible for all foster children who have been placed with the foster carer since their last review or since their approval. The regulations also state the FSP must 'make such enquires and obtain such information as they consider necessary in order to review whether the foster parent continues to be suitable to be a foster parent and the foster parent's household continues to be suitable' (DfE, 2011b, Regulation 28 (3)(a)). To obtain such information might involve seeking a wider set of views than just those that are suggested above. The UKNSFC, which are not mandatory but provide detail about foster carer reviews, suggest in addition to the SSW's report seeking: 'the written views of each social worker responsible for any child placed in the foster home since the last review, the views of children who are fostered and their parents where appropriate, and the views of the carer, her and his sons and daughters and any other household members' (UK Joint Working Party on Foster Care, 1999a, p46). In addition to this, Mehmet recommends that members of a foster carer's support network also make a contribution as well as 'anyone else who can provide evidence..., e.g. teachers of the children' (2005, p109), thus enabling third party evidence to be gathered.

To review and evaluate the quality of a foster carer's practice, their continuing suitability to be a foster carer and the appropriateness of their current terms of approval, there needs to be triangulation of evidence. This means that, for best practice, written reports must be sought from some individuals and should be sought from others. As required by regulation, the following must be gathered prior to the review meeting:

- the SSW's report;

- the foster carer's report;

- the views of all foster children placed with the foster carer (where possible in report form);

- the views of foster children's social workers for all foster children (where possible in report form).

Good practice would dictate that the following should be added to this list:

- the views of all foster children who were in placement during the review period but have moved on (where possible in report form);

- the foster carer's own children's views (where possible in report form);

- the foster children's parent's views (where this is appropriate and where possible in report form);

- third party views, for example, from a foster child's school, nursery, health visitor, etc (where possible in report form).

Structure and format for the review reports

FSPs currently use a range of different structures and formats for foster carer annual review reports. In 2014, BAAF developed the Form FR (England), which some agencies now use for undertaking their foster carer reviews (Adams, 2014). Adams' Form FR guidance is detailed, helpful and informative and complements this publication. Reports that are submitted from the different parties making a contribution to the foster carer's review need to be meaningful for those completing them as well as for the purposes of the review. For example, this will necessarily require the SSW's report's structure and format to be different from a foster child's report. Some FSPs have developed imaginative age-appropriate review forms for foster children and foster carer's own children to complete that incorporate drawings and the use of symbols as well as them offering a child the opportunity to make their own individual contributions. A foster child might not want to or be able to complete their own form because of their age or their ability. In such cases, either the SSW or the foster child's own social worker needs to interview them and record accurately their responses to questions and any of the child's own comments. It should not be left to the foster carer to complete this with their foster child.

Variation in report structure can be a strength but we need to make sure that all reviews incorporate areas that should be included. Each report's structure and format should be considered from the perspective of the person who is being asked to complete the report. In Chapter 6, I look in more detail at how to gather information for reviews and discuss some of the complexities of eliciting information from the different contributors. Here I address only the review administration form.

The foster carer review administration form

This form usefully includes the following:

- A cover sheet identifying all reports that should be part of the review paperwork and whether or not they are present. If a report is missing, there should be an explanation as to why.

- The foster carer's details.

- A brief profile of the foster carer and their household.

- The dates of the foster carer's approval, their fostering agreement and their reviews.

- Their current terms of approval.

- The minutes of the last panel that considered the foster carer's last review or their approval, if a first review.

- Any placements that were made that were outside the foster carer's terms of approval where an exemption was sought with dates and details of authorisation.

- The dates of the SSW's visits to the foster home.

- The dates of the SSW's supervision with the foster carer.

- The dates of unannounced visit/s made to the foster home.

- The dates of all statutory checks including the foster carer's Disclosure and Barring Service (DBS) check and LA check.

- The date of the foster carer's last medical.

- A list of the foster carer's DBS checked support network.

- An up-to-date and accurate list of each of the placements that a foster carer has had since their approval. Placements since their last review can be emboldened or italicised. This list should include the name of the foster child's social worker and in the case of IFPs also the foster child's local authority.

- A copy of the most recent health and safety report undertaken for the foster carer's home including any related actions. The most recent pet questionnaire where required.

- A copy of the foster carer's personal development plan including the training that they have undertaken since their approval or their last review. Date of completion or progress on completion of the CWDC's Standards workbook and plan to complete.

- A copy of the safer caring policy for the foster children placed and/or for the foster carer's household.

- The targets set from the foster carer's last review.

FOSTER CARER REVIEWS' RELATIONSHIP TO THE FOSTERING PANEL PROCESSES

FSPs have adopted various practices regarding foster carer reviews and their relationship to fostering panels. All first review reports have to be seen by the fostering panel (DfE, 2011b). It is then up to the FSP if and when subsequent reviews are seen by the fostering panel. Some FSPs present all their foster carer reviews to their fostering panel.

After the foster carer's first review has been seen by the fostering panel, some FSPs send foster carers' reviews to the fostering panel on a three-yearly cycle unless there is a particular reason that the FSP thinks that a review should be seen more frequently. As a bare minimum, which is above the current regulatory requirement, it is considered good practice for fostering panels to see foster carer reviews after their first review and thereafter every three years, unless circumstances require a review to be seen by the fostering panel sooner. Where a FSP can manage their resources in such a way that enables the fostering panel to see a foster carer's review annually, then that can only be a good thing.

There are FSPs which have adopted a practice whereby, in the year that a foster carer's review is due to be considered by the fostering panel, a review meeting is not held but rather a paper exercise is undertaken gathering together the review paperwork. The foster carer is invited to the panel and the panel is conducted as if it was undertaking the review meeting. This practice is problematic as a proper in-depth exploration about the quality of a foster carer's practice cannot be conducted in a fostering panel forum. 'Although there is no legal requirement to involve a reviewing officer or to hold a review meeting, any process that does not have this in place will be unable to achieve the full benefits of a comprehensive foster carer review' (Adams, 2014, p36). For good practice a review meeting should be conducted annually, chaired by an RO whether or not a foster carer's review is to be considered by a fostering panel. In line with the UKNSFC, this is what is meant by a "review": 'A review meeting is held that includes the carer, the supervising social worker and is chaired by an appropriate third party' (UK Joint Working Party on Foster Care, 1999a, p46). The RO then completes their report which is collated with the other reports prepared for the review. This is the review documentation that is submitted to the FSP and/or the fostering panel.

SUMMARY

To reiterate, the suggested review administrative process should be as follows.

- The review administrator keeps and regularly updates a database of the FSP's foster carers including the name of the foster carer, the date of their approval, their SSW, their SSW's manager, the RO, the date of their last review and the date of their next review.

- Newly-approved foster carers' details are added to the review database and a provisional date for their review is set for 11 months after their approval. Once a foster child is placed with the foster carer, a new date can be set within six months after the foster child's placement started, if that date is sooner than the first provisional date.

- Eight weeks before the review date the review administrator sends the SSW all the review forms for completion. It is the responsibility of the SSW and their manager to make sure that all these forms are completed by the relevant parties and returned to the review administrator two weeks prior to the review meeting date.

- When they have received all the paperwork, the review administrator collates the papers into one document with numbered pages.

- The review administrator, in consultation with the SSW, then updates the foster carer review administration form (outlined above) which becomes the first section of the collated documentation.

- The collated documentation is then checked by the SSW's manager and signed off by them before it is sent to the RO to read. This enables the RO to devise an annotated agenda to use when chairing the review meeting.

- Once the review meeting has been held, the RO writes their RO's report and sends it to the SSW, the SSW's manager and the review administrator (within a suggested maximum of three weeks after the review meeting).

- The RO's report should be read by the SSW and their manager, checking for factual accuracy. The RO might have different views and conclusions from the SSW and their manager but these should not be altered. The reading and checking of the report is for factual matters only. Any changes that the SSW and their manager suggest should be agreed with the RO.

- The RO's report is then collated into the overall review documentation ready for the review document to be read by the FSP's ADM and/or the fostering panel, depending on the nature of the review and whether or not it is a first review.

- The collated review documentation, the minutes of the fostering panel relating to the particular foster carer's review (when the review has been considered by the fostering panel), and a copy of the FSP's ADM's letter to the foster carer regarding the outcome of their review should be filed in the foster carer's file both electronically as well as in hard copy.

6

Information gathering for reviews

INTRODUCTION

Chapter 5 looked at the collection and collation of foster carer review paperwork from the angle of administrative efficiency. This chapter looks at how to gain meaningful contributions from people who can usefully comment on a foster carer's work. Adams' (2014) detailed guidance on information gathering and analysis for foster carer reviews complements this chapter.

The chapter is organised into two sections. The first section looks at the SSW's and the foster carer's reports, the first being an evaluative report and the second being a self-evaluative report. The second section addresses how best to gain meaningful contributions from other key players in the foster carer review process.

THE SSW'S AND THE FOSTER CARER'S REPORTS

The social worker's evaluative report and the foster carer's self-evaluative report, however structured, need to address the foster carer's capacity to facilitate a foster child's overall development and the TSDS requirements (if in England) (DfE, 2012a). It is vital that a holistic appraisal of a foster carer's work and the story of their foster care provided for the foster child since their last review or their approval for first reviews (the review period) is not lost in making sure all the above are covered. In addition to these aspects that must be covered, in both the SSW's and the foster carer's reports, I have set out below areas that I think ought to be covered and could possibly be missed by just adhering to the above.

At the time of writing, some FSPs still use the ECM five "outcomes" to structure the SSW's evaluative report, others the NMS, the TSDS or the

BAAF Form FR. Whatever the structure, the FSP needs to be mindful of how all DfE guidance and regulation requirements are evidenced.

At the present time, foster carers' and SSWs' review paperwork tends to be divided into two sections. In some FSPs, the SSW and the foster carer complete reports that appraise the foster carer's overall fostering practice for the review period. In addition, they complete separate reports about the foster care provided for each child who has been placed within the review period. For other FSPs, these two reports (the appraisal of the review period and the reports on the care of individual foster children) are amalgamated into a single report by the foster carer and one by the SSW. Regardless of the way in which the paperwork is organised, each specific foster child's placement, their individual experience of being placed with the foster carer, and the quality of the foster care they received needs to be evaluated by the foster carer and the SSW.

I have covered the SSW report in more detail than the foster carer report. This is not to downgrade the foster carer report but rather to emphasise the statutory duties involved in foster carer reviews – that it is the foster carer who is being reviewed and the SSW's professional judgement about the quality of their foster care that is being deployed. The review is also an opportunity for the foster carer to evaluate their own practice and plan with their SSW their continuing development over the next period.

THE SSW'S EVALUATIVE REPORT

The SSW's report is evaluative. This means that the SSW is required to analyse and synthesise the material they present in their report to enable: evidence-based judgements to be made about the quality of the foster carer's work; whether or not they and their household continue to be suitable to foster; and, if so, whether or not their current terms of approval are still appropriate.

In the usual course of events reviews take place annually or, as recommended in this guide, six months after a foster child is placed with a newly-approved foster carer. However, an FSP can conduct a review at any time they see fit and at whatever frequency as long as the minimum regulatory requirements are met (DfE, 2011b, 2013a). Additional reviews are usually triggered by an allegation or a complaint that has been made about a carer or where there has been a change of circumstances for the foster carer and/or their household. The investigation of an allegation or a complaint should be conducted separately from the review. It is most productive to conduct the review once the investigations have been completed. However, this is subject to the regulatory timeframes being met.

Content

As noted above, the SSW's report needs to address the quality of the foster carer's care of each individual child and appraise the quality of their overall foster care. These requirements can be met in separate reports or within one report.

However sophisticated the format of the SSW's report, its usefulness will depend on the SSW's ability to evidence their report and analyse the material they draw on in such a way that identifies strengths, areas for further development, patterns and concerns. This will enable sound judgements to be made about the quality of the fostering undertaken in the review period. The SSW's reports must be literate, fluent, detailed, logical and contain evidence of reasoned analysis leading to a recommendation. Evidenced decision making should be apparent as should the ability to differentiate fact from opinion. The Wakefield inquiry identified failings in one of the SSW's reports presented for the foster carers' first review in that it lacked sufficient analysis and failed to identify worrying emerging patterns (Parrott *et al*, 2007). To enable the identification of both worrying as well as positive patterns, the SSW has to be familiar with the content of the foster carer's original Form F assessment report and their subsequent review reports.

The SSW's report, whatever the format used, in addition to the above will need to cover the following.

Current circumstances

SSW reports have to cover the foster carer's current circumstances. If there have been any significant changes to the foster carer's own circumstances or to those of members of their household or to the household's composition during the review period, these need to be noted and, most importantly, the implications for fostering explored.

The fostering story

This section includes the placement story for each foster child placed with the foster carer during the review period. The SSW's report should provide chronologically the narrative of each placement. The narrative section enables all the parties, including the RO, to gain a holistic understanding of the foster carer's work during the review period.

The fostering household and its dynamics

The quality of the relationships within the fostering household and what the impact of these relationships has been on foster children should be considered in the SSW's report. This includes addressing the quality of the relationship of a fostering couple (where there is a couple fostering), the foster carer's relationship with their own children (where there are foster carer's own children), and the relationships between their own children and the foster child. The SSW should also describe the lifestyle of the fostering household. For example, what sort of activities do they do with the foster child, what is the structure of an average weekday and the weekend? The implications for the foster child of the family's lifestyle should be addressed. When there is a couple fostering, the report needs to address both of their fostering roles and responsibilities and the quality of their individual foster care as well as how they foster as a couple.

The SSW should describe the foster carer's home and state whether or not, in their professional judgement, it is a suitable environment for a foster child. They need to consider what the home feels like from the perspective of a foster child: is it warm and welcoming? This will require the SSW to be familiar with the whole house and garden (where there is one) and importantly, the foster child's bedroom. This professional judgement about the home as a suitable environment for a foster child is in addition to the health and safety checks and the safer care policies for the fostering household and/or each of the foster children. It is more about such things as: the care taken of a foster child's bedroom; what toys and/or equipment the foster child has; how individualised their bedroom is; where a foster child does their homework; where a 17-year-old fostered young person can study quietly when revising for their exams.

The impact of fostering on the foster carer and their family

The SSW's report must include an appraisal of how a foster carer's family and members of their household have experienced fostering during the review period. This assessment will be informed by the work that the SSW has done with the foster carer's family but also from the reports that family members will have individually completed for the purposes of the review.

Highlights of the review period

Foster carer reviews are primarily about the FSP making sure that a foster carer is still appropriate as such and that the care they are providing to foster children is of a good standard. Reviews also offer the opportunity to address with the foster carer what they have done particularly well. It is important that throughout the year the SSW gathers evidence of the foster carer's abilities and achievements that can be presented at the review stage.

Complaints and/or allegations

SSW reports need to explicitly address any concerns about, complaints or allegations against a foster carer that have arisen during the review period. It is helpful to have a section of the SSW's report that directly requires the SSW to address this area and records the outcomes of any investigations or complaints processes.

Importantly issues or concerns raised in the previous review as well as any matters raised by the fostering panel, where applicable, should also be addressed.

The quality of the foster carer's relationship with and direct care of foster children

Reviews must directly address the most fundamentally important aspect of fostering, that being the quality of the direct care of foster children. The RO will be reliant on the SSW's evaluation. This includes evidence that a foster carer ensures that a foster child is well clothed, eats healthy fresh food, is up to date with their medicals, visits to the optician and dentist, has an established routine, is encouraged educationally as well as with their hobbies and leisure pursuits, etc. The SSW must comment on a foster carer's ability to: show warmth and affection to a foster child; enjoy the company of children; play with a foster child at an age-appropriate level; talk to a child or young person; set appropriate boundaries for a foster child to enable them to feel and be safe and cared for and facilitate changes in a foster child's behaviour where this is needed using evidence-based approaches that are both kind and containing.

The SSW should comment on the foster carer's capacity to understand the impact of loss, transition and change on a foster child and to empathetically engage with them. For example, this can be evidenced by how a foster carer helps a child manage their feelings and behaviour stimulated by contact with a member of their birth family or how they helped them settle into their home the first night they were placed.

The foster carer's ability to respect and value the familial, racial, national, linguistic, cultural and religious heritage of a child should be commented on within the SSW's report. This "comment" should be more than just providing evidence that the foster carer has provided appropriate physical care and food for a foster child and facilitated them locating the nearest place of worship appropriate to their religion (where relevant). Rather, the SSW's appraisal should be about how the foster carer conveyed their interest in, respect for and engagement with the foster child's family, their history, their language, their country of origin, their religion and their culture.

The SSW's reports must include their direct observations of the quality of a foster carer's relationship with the foster child. The SSW will have a wealth of material to draw on from their visits to the foster home. For example, how did the foster carer comfort, play with, talk to a foster child and/or manage their behaviour on a particular occasion observed by the SSW?

The foster carer's facilitation of contact

A foster carer will usually be involved with their foster child's contact with their birth family. Dependent on the nature of the care plan for the foster child, this involvement will range from, for example, taking a child five times a week to a contact centre to facilitating contact between their foster child and their parent in the foster carer's home on Saturdays. The SSW needs to evidence and appraise how a foster carer has facilitated contact for their foster child. How effectively have they worked with their foster child, their parent/s, the professionals involved and the contact centre? Contact can be complicated and stressful for foster carers. Research evidence suggests that a child's social worker's input and the SSW's supervision and support can help foster carers to manage related stress and help make contact more effective for foster children (Austerberry et al, 2013; Brown et al, 2014). It is therefore helpful to consider how the FSP and the SSW have supervised and supported the foster carer around their foster child's contact and if that support and supervision have been useful.

Delegated authority

Where delegated authority (DfE, 2013b) has been agreed in relation to the care of a foster child, the SSW needs to comment on how effectively the foster carer has worked with the related agreements.

The quality of the foster carer's relationship with the FSP

The quality of the working relationship between the SSW, the foster carer and the FSP was identified in the Wakefield inquiry to be a significant factor that was insufficiently explored in the foster carers' review (Parrott et al, 2007). The quality of the working relationship is crucial for effective communication and for making sure that a foster child is kept safe and that their needs are met.

In addition to a record of the dates of unannounced visits being visible in the foster carer review administration form, the SSW should comment on these visits as they provide a snapshot of a foster carer's home, their lifestyle and the day-to-day experience of living in that foster home for foster children. However, they only ever provide a snapshot.

In addition, the SSW should evaluate the foster carer's ability to meet all the bureaucratic requirements of the FSP. These will include keeping financial records of how money is spent on the care of a foster child and the quality of a foster carer's recordings about the foster child. Importantly, the SSW's report has to evaluate the foster carer's ability to use supervision effectively and apply what they have learnt to the direct care of a foster child.

The foster carer's relationship with other professionals

Foster care is primarily about the direct care of foster children, enabling their development, and helping them reach their potential. Being an effective foster carer also requires the ability to work with a range of other professionals involved with the foster child and this ability should be explicitly evaluated in the SSW's report.

The effectiveness of the foster carer's support network

The review administration form should list members of the foster carer's support network who are DBS checked by the FSP. The SSW needs to appraise the effectiveness of this support network and comment on how it has been utilised within the review period. If the support network's composition needs reviewing, that should be identified as a target for the SSW and the foster carer and discussed at the review meeting.

The foster carer's personal development plan

The SSW needs to comment on the foster carer's personal development plan including training they have attended during the review period and how the training has been utilised by the foster carer in their direct care of foster children. The SSW's report should include a plan, agreed with the foster carer, about the foster carer's continuing development for the forthcoming year including what training they will attend. There needs to be explicit reference to the TSDS (DfE, 2012a; Adams, 2014; Brown, 2014b).

Targets to be achieved before the next review

The SSW's report should include targets for themselves, the FSP and the foster carer for the forthcoming year as well as information about how targets set from the foster carer's last review have been realised.

Areas for discussion at the review meeting

The SSW must identify specific matters to be discussed at the review meeting.

Recommendation

The SSW's report should logically progress towards a properly substantiated and evidenced recommendation regarding a foster carer's suitability to continue to be approved as a foster carer and whether or not their terms of approval should remain the same or be changed. If they are recommending that the foster carer's terms of approval should be changed, they need to state their reasons for this recommendation and if the foster carer is in agreement. If the SSW is not recommending the foster carer's continued approval, they need to set out their reasons and what work has been done to enable the foster carer to make the required changes to provide a balanced report which highlights strengths and concerns.

THE FOSTER CARER'S REPORT

The foster carer's report is self-evaluative and should describe and appraise the fostering undertaken during the review period. Some foster carers need support to complete their review paperwork and this should be provided where necessary by the FSP. However, it is likely, as a result of foster carers' completion of the TSDS portfolio (DfE, 2012a), that foster carers will be more familiar with self-evaluation than some had been hitherto.

Foster carers' reports ought to identify what they consider they have done well and where they feel they could improve. The reports should also identify how they think their SSW and their FSP could further support them in their foster care and their development, including the identification of relevant training.

As noted above, the foster carer will need to consider the care of each foster child whom they have cared for and/or continue to care for during the review period. The report/s that the foster carer is required to complete should also reference the TSDS requirements (Adams, 2014). In so doing, the narrative of the review period should not be lost, as noted above. The foster carer's report should include the same areas that I have identified for the SSW's report and consider the same detail identified above.

Content

- Current circumstances

- The fostering story

- The household and its dynamics

- The impact of fostering on the foster carer and their family

- Highlights of the review period

- Complaints and/or allegations

- The quality of the foster carer's relationship with and direct care of foster children

- The foster carer's facilitation of contact

- How the foster carer has managed the delegated authority arrangements for particular foster children

- The quality of the foster carer's relationship with the FSP

- The foster carer's relationship with other professionals

- The effectiveness of the foster carer's support network

- The foster carer's personal development plan

- Targets to be achieved before the next review

- Areas for discussion at the review meeting

- Terms of approval – the foster carer must be afforded the opportunity in writing to say if their current terms of approval still feel appropriate and if not, why. If they want their terms of approval changed, they should state what they would like them to be, putting an argument forward to back the request for the change.

FACILITATING CONTRIBUTORS' INPUT TO FOSTER CARER REVIEWS

It is usually the responsibility of the SSW to make sure that all contributors' reports for a foster carer's review are completed and returned to the review administrator by a set date. This requires the SSW to be tenacious in making sure that everyone completes and returns their reports on time. Unsuccessful efforts to obtain a foster child's social worker's comments could be followed up with the respective team manager to obtain, at the very least, verbal feedback that could be recorded.

Foster children's contributions

All foster children who are currently placed with a foster carer must be asked to make a contribution to the foster carer's review (DfE, 2011b). In addition, it is good practice to ask foster children who were placed with the foster carer during the review period but are no longer placed with them, for their contribution. FSPs have developed a range of child-friendly ways to elicit foster children's contributions to reviews. I use the term "contribution" as this can be made in different ways, not just through a written report. Best practice requires the FSP to clarify who facilitates the foster child's contribution – the SSW or the foster child's social worker? It is not appropriate for the foster carer to do this work with a foster child. The foster child needs to be familiar with whoever approaches them for their contribution. If a foster child has moved on to another placement during the review period, then it is best for the child's social worker to gain their views about their previous placement with the foster carer.

Whoever facilitates the foster child's contribution needs to consider whether the foster child would rather complete a review report form or be interviewed. This will be dependent on a number of factors, including the age of the child as well as their ability. FSPs sometimes cite the age of a child or their ability as reasons why a foster child has not made a contribution to a foster carer's review. Regulation and best practice require that, wherever possible, foster children should contribute to foster carer reviews. Young children and children who, for whatever reason, cannot or will not complete a review report form should be interviewed separately from their foster carer and their contribution accurately recorded.

A foster child's contribution to a foster carer's review is key to the overall evaluation of the quality of foster care being provided. The foster child's experience of being cared for by the foster carer is fundamentally important. Without their contribution the review will only ever be partial. The foster child needs to understand why they are completing a review report form or why they are being interviewed and how what they say or write will be used. They need to be engaged in an age-appropriate manner. There are helpful books looking at communicating with children and the best ways of helping children express what they think and feel (Luckock and Lefevre, 2008; Thomas, 2009; Lefevre, 2010). Although none of these texts specifically address foster children's contributions to foster carer reviews, they look at communicating with children from many different standpoints and usefully consider communication with disabled children, young children and adolescents and different media for communication including writing, drawing, games, play and talking. Communicating with children for some social workers raises anxiety as they feel they lack the necessary skills. Thomas helpfully reminds us that:

Communicating with children and young people is not necessarily so very different from communicating with adults. Wherever people are in need, the basic requirements are the same – warmth, empathy, trust, and sensitivity to the person's verbal and non-verbal language and style of communication.

(Thomas, 2009, p66)

If a foster child is being interviewed rather than completing a review report, the social worker recording the interview needs to say where the interview took place and note observations they made about the interview and the child's contribution. Thomas notes the importance of non-verbal communication when he writes: 'children's non-verbal communication can be just as important and revealing as their words, and sometimes more so' (Thomas, 2009, p66). This non-verbal communication should be noted and its significance analysed.

A foster child's contribution should focus on what their experience is/ was of being cared for by the foster carer. Such areas as: what it was like when they arrived at the foster carer's home; whether they were made welcome; what they think of their bedroom, their clothes, toys, equipment and the food they are given; what it is like living with the foster family; how the foster carer helps them keep in touch with their birth family (where appropriate); if they can talk to their foster carer about any worries they have or when they feel unhappy; how the foster carer helps them with their school work; and whom they would talk to if they were unhappy about something in their foster home. As a minimum requirement these are areas that should be covered with a foster child.

The foster child needs to be given the opportunity to say anything that they want to and should not be limited by the SSW's use of direct questions or by the format of a review report form they are completing. The report form and the SSW undertaking the interview should use open questions. It is useful to end an interview or a report form with a question such as 'is there anything else you would like to tell me about what it is/was like living with your foster carer?' thus enabling a foster child to make their own undirected contribution.

If a foster child is interviewed, this should take place somewhere where the foster child feels comfortable. Similarly, if a foster child is completing a review report form, thought needs to be given to how they will receive the form, and how the purpose of its completion will be properly explained. Some foster children want to complete their forms alone but others value their social worker or the SSW being with them so they can discuss what they are writing. FSPs might explore the possibility of a foster child submitting their contribution by email where appropriate. FSPs should be mindful that some foster children have "report completion fatigue"; this might be the tenth form they have been asked to complete over the years for the same purpose.

The foster carer's own children's contributions

Foster carers' own children should be given the opportunity to contribute to reviews. Höjer and colleagues, in their international literature review about the impact of fostering on foster carers' own children, argue that:

The children and young people in carers' families need to be involved in family discussions concerning the decision to foster and should not be seen as less significant, passive members of the family. The evidence from this review suggests that fostering will have an impact on their lives and they need to understand how and in what ways they will be affected.

(2013, p5)

It follows that foster carers' children need to be actively engaged in their parents' annual reviews in order to contribute their thinking about being part of a fostering family. The same applies to these children as I have noted above for foster children. They need to be asked to make their contribution about what their experience is living in a fostering family through whatever medium is considered the most appropriate for them as individuals. The following are important to include: whom they would talk to if they were unhappy about anything related to fostering or a foster child? What are the good things about being in a fostering family and what are the less good things?

The impact of fostering on a foster carer's own children is an important consideration for a FSP. There might be times where the needs of a foster carer's own child should be the main focus for the foster carer and they need to take a break from fostering to focus on their own child. The needs and circumstances of foster carer's own children are areas that must be explicitly addressed in the review process as well as at the review meeting.

The foster children's social worker's contributions for all foster children placed during the review period

Regulations require foster children's social workers to contribute to the foster carer's review (DfE, 2011b). Social workers' views are important to inform the review meeting about the quality of foster care that their foster child received or is receiving. They will be able to comment on the foster carer's ability to work with the foster child's birth family around contact and the foster carer's ability to work with other professionals. For example, the foster child's social worker will have observed at first hand the foster carer's contributions to a foster child's looked after children's review.

The foster child's social worker's contribution to a foster carer's review has been shown to be important in Chapter 3. Their views are sometimes different from the SSW's and exploring differing viewpoints in the review meeting can be important for informing safe decision making. Adams makes the important point that:

> Hearing from the person who effectively commissions the foster care on behalf of the child means that any collusion (deliberate or unintended) between the supervising social worker and the foster carer to present things as better than they are is not possible, and that if the child feels unable to fully set out their concerns (as they are living in that home), then their social worker can do it for them. In this respect, the child's social worker has a crucial safeguarding responsibility.

(2014, p28)

Foster children's social workers are usually busy and under pressure and might not see the completion of a report for a review as a priority. The SSW needs to pursue the foster child's social worker by email and telephone to make sure the report is completed. Where a report is not forthcoming, this needs to be dealt with by the FSP's senior managers as the foster child's social worker's input is required by regulation.

The foster child's parent's contributions (where appropriate)

Best practice dictates that contributions from a foster child's parent/s about what they think of the quality of care their child has received or is receiving should be sought where possible. Their views will improve the depth of evaluation about the quality of the foster care being provided. In the sub-title of this section I have written "(where appropriate)". This is because there might be specific circumstances when seeking the contribution of a foster child's parent/s would not be in a foster child's interest. However, these circumstances are rare. In the majority of cases, parents do not make contributions to foster carers' reviews because they are not asked. Where they are asked and they make a contribution, it is often helpful and useful to the review process. A parent might raise a pertinent matter of which no other contributor to the review process is aware. Gaining their views adds to a holistic evaluation of a foster carer's work and increases the possibility of triangulation of evidence to inform professional judgements and decision making.

Some parents might not want to complete a written review report form and should be offered the opportunity of being interviewed face-to-face or on the telephone or submitting their contribution by email (where appropriate). Standard 16.2 of the UKNSFC noted that the written views of the parent of a foster child (where appropriate) should be sought for a foster carer's review (UK Joint Working Party on Foster Care, 1999a, p46). The Government has reiterated, in its guidance for care planning, placement and case review, the importance of working in partnership with parents. The guidance states that 'parents should be expected and enabled to retain their responsibilities and to remain as closely involved as is consistent with their child's welfare, even if that child cannot live at home either temporarily or permanently' (DCSF, 2010, p3). The guidance goes on to state that, in line with the intention of the Children Act 1989, 'parents should be encouraged to exercise their responsibility for their child's welfare in a constructive way...' (DCSF, 2010, p3). In the spirit of this guidance, it is important to gain a foster child's parent's views about the quality of the foster care that their child receives.

Third parties' contributions

The regulations state that a FSP must 'make such enquires and obtain such information as they consider necessary in order to review whether the foster parent continues to be suitable to be a foster parent and the foster parent's household continues to be suitable' (DfE, 2011b, reg 28(1)(a)). It is therefore necessary for the SSW to seek third party evidence to inform the review process. It is good practice to supply at least one third party report commenting on the foster care that has been provided. For example, reports can be sought from the foster child's school, nursery, the foster child's Children's Guardian; a CAMHS psychologist; the foster child's Youth Offending Service social worker or from their college tutor; whoever can make a meaningful evaluative contribution. Where a foster carer has done a particular piece of work, such as introducing a foster child to their prospective adoptive parent/s, a report from the adoptive parents is useful.

Where there have been specific concerns raised by a third party (for example, the school, health visitor, nursery) about the foster carer or the standard of care provided, the SSW should seek a report from that party to inform the review.

Where a foster child's own child has experienced difficulties within the review period, then third party reports relating to the impact of those difficulties on the suitability of the fostering household to continue to care for foster children should be sought.

The contribution that third party reports make can be invaluable and give a different perspective to those of the foster carer, the foster child, the SSW and the foster child's social worker.

SUMMARY

For foster carers' reviews to be meaningful and for informed, safe recommendations to be made regarding whether or not a foster carer should continue to foster, there needs to be sufficient breadth of contributions. SSW and their FSPs should give enough time to the process of gathering review reports from contributors and make sure that their own evaluative report is considered, well-evidenced and that its conclusions and recommendations flow logically from the analysis within the report.

When the reports are finally collected and collated, the review paperwork should be sent to the RO so they can prepare for chairing the review meeting.

7

The review meeting

INTRODUCTION

The review meeting itself is central to the review process (Adams, 2014; Brown, 2014a, 2014b). It is where matters arising from the review reports can be properly explored. The deliberations of the review meeting and the content of the review reports inform the RO's report and their recommendation regarding the foster carer's continuing approval as a foster carer and their terms of approval.

All foster carer reviews should have a review meeting conducted which is separate from the fostering panel process and which takes place before the final review paperwork is submitted to the FSP and/or the fostering panel. Adams argues the importance of the review meeting being an opportunity for rigorous scrutiny when he writes:

> *The review must be a robust meeting that serves as an important quality assurance mechanism for the fostering service, but it needs to be much more than a series of checklists, and to be useful needs to allow for in-depth discussion and reflection.*

(2014, p37)

The review meeting should be chaired by someone other than the SSW or the SSW's manager. The UKNSFC Standard 16.6 states that: 'A review meeting is held that includes the carer and the supervising social worker, and is chaired by an appropriate third party, who can form an independent judgement and is knowledgeable about foster care' (UK Joint Working Party on Foster Care, 1999, p46). Many FSPs use independent social workers as ROs to chair foster carer reviews. Others use senior members of the FSP who do not have line management responsibility for the foster carer and yet others draw from their pool of IROs for looked after children. Where FSPs use IROs for the purposes of the foster carer RO role, they need to be mindful of the Wakefield inquiry recommendation that for the foster carer review 'the Chair should not be the same person who chairs reviews on the children who have been placed with the carers' (Parrott *et al*, 2007, p141).

To maximise the possibility of an "independent judgement" being reached, wherever possible an RO should ideally be drawn from outside the FSP as they are more likely to be able to maintain an independent stance. That is not to say that ROs drawn from the FSPs cannot form independent judgements. The most important factor to consider when identifying an RO to chair a foster carer review meeting is the capability of that RO. The only publication that addresses this is the Wakefield inquiry and only in as much as the inquiry team recounted the RO's deficits. The inquiry report noted the importance of an RO's ability to 'facilitate, analysis and weighing up information before arriving at a conclusion' (Parrott *et al*, 2007, p92). The RO should have the skills and knowledge to:

- critically read the review paperwork sent to them prior to the review meeting taking place;

- identify salient areas that should be discussed at the review meeting and any matters that need to be explored with relevant parties beforehand;

- formulate an agenda covering pertinent areas for all foster carer review meetings as well as particular matters related to the specific foster carer;

- chair the meeting in a facilitative, inclusive and rigorous manner;

- draw out key matters explored in the review meeting; and

- write a RO's report that is analytic, logical and makes a substantiated and properly evidenced recommendation drawing on the deliberations of the review meeting as well as the review paperwork.

PREPARATIONS FOR THE REVIEW MEETING

The review paperwork should be sent to the RO by the foster carer review administrator at least a week prior to the review meeting taking place. This gives the RO enough time to read the paperwork, raise any queries and seek clarification. The foster carer and the SSW should have their own copies of the review paperwork so that they can prepare for the meeting. Best practice dictates that the RO should be familiar with the foster carer's original assessment report and any subsequent amended assessment reports (for example, where there has been a re-assessment because of a foster carer establishing a relationship with a new partner) as well as with the paperwork from the previous review including the previous RO's report and the related fostering panel minutes where this is applicable. Reading this material enables the RO to identify both positive and negative themes and patterns that might be emerging through the foster carer's practice.

The RO should read the review paperwork critically and analytically thus enabling the identification of key areas to be explored during or prior to the review meeting. In so doing it is important that they identify any missing reports and seek clarification as to why they are missing if this explanation is not present in the SSW's report or the review administration form. The RO needs to: become familiar with the content of the review paperwork and each of its component parts; identify any contradictory comments; identify gaps in what has been commented upon, for example, there might have been no mention made of the foster carer's ability to facilitate a foster child's involvement in leisure activities or the quality of their relationship with a foster child's birth family or how they are gathering mementoes from the placement for their foster child; identify any emerging themes; make sure that all regulatory requirements have been met including all necessary checks being up to date and that targets from the previous review or those set by the approval panel or the panel that considered the foster carer's last review have been realised. They should identify good fostering practice and where the foster carer has developed as well as noting areas of concern.

Foster carer ROs will have different ways of preparing for chairing review meetings. Whatever the approach, ROs need to plan an agenda for the review meeting which addresses specific matters arising from the review paperwork. Some ROs follow an agenda which replicates the RO's report headings used by the FSP. If this is the approach, it is the RO's responsibility to make sure that the agenda is sufficiently individualised and pertinent to the specific foster carer's review, thus avoiding a formulaic tick box approach that might lead to important areas being missed.

On reading the review paperwork, the RO might identify further work that needs to be undertaken prior to the review meeting or that they need to seek clarification about a particular matter raised or an opinion voiced. For example, the RO might want to ask for a comment made by a teacher in a report submitted by a foster child's school to be expanded upon. It is best that requests for clarification or additional information from contributors to the review are channelled through the SSW or their manager so that lines of responsibility remain clear.

When the RO reads the review paperwork and it becomes apparent that a matter needs to be addressed prior to the review meeting itself, they must discuss this with the SSW and the SSW manager. For example, a radically different view reported by a foster child's social worker and the SSW about the quality of care provided to a foster child would need exploration prior to the review meeting. In such cases, as was recommended in the Wakefield inquiry, the RO should ask that this be explored and clarified by the FSP prior to the review meeting.

THE REVIEW MEETING

The purpose of the review meeting is for the RO, the foster carer and the SSW to evaluate and appraise the foster care that has been undertaken during the review period. The RO should have the requisite interpersonal and chairing skills to enable the foster carer to participate in the review in such a way that enables them to feel respected and valued. It is their review. Where there have been concerns raised about the quality of their fostering, they must have the opportunity to give their perspective and feel that this has been explored and noted. Having read the review paperwork, the RO can offer an independent appraisal of the work that has been undertaken.

The review meeting should be held in the foster carer's home. When a couple are approved as foster carers, both carers must be present at the review meeting as they are both being reviewed. The RO might ask that other members of the fostering household be present for all or part of the review meeting to better inform the discussion, evaluation and resulting recommendation. At the beginning of the review meeting, the RO should make sure that the foster carer understands the regulatory requirements for foster carer reviews. The RO needs to make clear that they make a recommendation regarding a foster carer's continuing approval and their terms of approval and that recommendation goes to the fostering panel and/or the FSP. The final decision is made by the FSP's ADM. If there are concerns raised in the review paperwork that might lead to a possible recommendation of terminating a foster carer's approval, this needs to be made explicit to the foster carer by the FSP prior to the review meeting. In such cases a FSP might make the decision that the SSW's manager should also attend the review meeting.

The RO role requires good interpersonal and chairing skills as well as the ability to think in a critical and reflective way to enable an open, honest, rigorous and foster child-focused discussion. The RO needs to be mindful of both the content as well as the process of the review meeting. It is often the case that, as well as chairing the review meeting, the RO makes notes about what is said. If this is done, the RO needs to explain to the foster carer why they are taking notes and how the notes will be used. It is good practice for the RO to thank the foster carer and the SSW for their contributions to the review paperwork and their work in preparing for the review.

Whatever the preferred review meeting agenda, it is the RO's responsibility to make sure that all necessary areas are covered in the review meeting and that the following areas are discussed and explored:

- the review period;

- any changes to the foster carer's circumstances, or to the composition of their household;

- significant events for the foster carer and their family;

- each placement story for each of the foster children placed during the review period. As well as a holistic review, this should include: the quality of the direct care of each of the foster children, including the foster carer's emotional and physical care of the foster child, and how they have managed any problematic behaviour and facilitated the foster child's overall development;

- where the foster carer has their own children, how those children are doing and what the impact is on them of being part of a fostering family;

- the quality of the working relationship between the foster carer and the SSW and the FSP;

- the quality of the working relationships between the foster carer and other professionals involved with the foster children placed during the review period;

- the quality of the foster carer's involvement with a foster child's contact arrangements and with their birth family and their ability to help a child make sense of their circumstances and their placement story;

- the use made and effectiveness of the foster carer's DBS checked support network;

- the foster carer's personal development plan including what training and education they have undertaken and how their learning has been utilised with foster children placed with them during the review period. For first reviews, the foster carer's completion of the TSDS (DfE, 2012a) needs to be checked and a plan made regarding the completion of the related workbook if this has still to be finished;

- any allegations or complaints investigation's outcomes and their implications for the foster carer's continued approval;

- that all checks required by regulations and medical checks are up to date and that any identified required actions from the most recent annual health and safety check on the foster carer's home are being dealt with;

- that the safer care policy for the foster family and/or specific foster children is up to date and effective;

- targets from the foster carer's last review and matters raised in fostering panel minutes;

- targets to be set for the period before the next review;

- the recommendation and the terms of approval and the rationale for both;

- summing up: identifying areas of strengths, concerns and areas for further development;

- the date of the next review.

During the review, the RO has the opportunity to meet the foster carer and hear their perspectives on the review period and their evaluation of the quality of the work they have done as well as hearing the SSW's views. The foster carer and the SSW might want to provide evidence at the review meeting of excellent or good fostering practice. For example, a foster carer might have facilitated a successful introduction of an 18-month-old child to prospective adopters in the review period. As a result of the quality of this work, they might have written to the foster carers thanking them for their work, which gave the adopters a solid beginning to their relationship with their adopted child. Showing this letter to the RO is helpful as it can be drawn on in the RO's report as evidence of an effective piece of work that the foster carer has undertaken.

The RO can ask the foster carer to describe particular events as a way of exploring the quality of their practice. For example: how did the foster carer manage the arrival of a particular foster child? How was that child welcomed? How does the foster carer think the child felt when they arrived and by the time they went to bed? These discussions can help flesh out a foster carer's ability to empathise with a foster child and throw light on their understanding of the emotional impact of separation, loss and transition on a foster child and how they enabled a child to feel safe enough, both physically and emotionally.

How the foster carer managed a foster child's problematic behaviour is important to discuss in the review meeting. Exploring the detail of what the foster carer did to manage such behaviour and their understanding of the foster child's actions as well as the effectiveness of their response is helpful. The content of the SSW's supervision should be discussed to ascertain that the foster carer is getting support and advice that is based on research evidence about what works in helping children with their behaviour, for example, approaches drawn from social learning theory and utilised in such training programmes as *Fostering Changes* (Warman, 2006; Briskman *et al*, 2013; Bachmann *et al*, 2014).

Where foster children have moved on in a planned way, the RO should explore if there are any unresolved areas for the foster carer. Where the foster carer was strongly attached to a foster child, the RO should ascertain if they got support that enabled a successful transition for the foster child and a satisfactory ending for themselves. Where a foster carer has precipitated an unplanned ending to a foster child's placement, the circumstances from the perspective of the foster carer, the SSW and the FSP need to be discussed and any implications for future placements considered. The review meeting offers the opportunity for differences of opinion to be aired and addressed.

In the review meeting the RO can help identify the foster carer's strengths, concerns and where further development is needed. The RO has the opportunity to listen to the foster carer's detailed description of their care of and relationship with the foster child. It is important that the RO is sensitive to affect, gaps and themes that emerge. For example, it might become apparent that the foster carer speaks with warmth about a particular foster child but not with such affection when talking about that foster child's older sister whom they also foster. If such material is evident in the review meeting, it is the RO's responsibility to identify it so that the quality of the foster carer's relationships with their foster children can be fully discussed. The RO must explore all areas identified in the paperwork that raise concern, lack clarity or are contradictory.

As the review meeting is conducted in the foster carer's home, this means that sometimes foster children and the foster carer's own children might be at home at the time the review meeting is held. Where this is the case, the foster carer should make sure that the children are occupied so that the review meeting can go ahead and that discussions that might be concerning for foster children or birth children are not overheard. Sometimes review meetings will be interrupted by a domestic matter, such as a 14-year-old wanting a snack or needing help to find their iPhone before they go off to visit a friend. It is the RO's responsibility to make sure that, even when there are unavoidable interruptions, the review meeting remains properly chaired and follows the agenda so that all areas can be sufficiently addressed.

The RO's observational skills need to be deployed during the review meeting. The RO has the opportunity to observe firsthand the quality of the relationship between the foster carer and the SSW and, where there is a foster child at home, the quality of the relationship between the foster carer and the foster child. Where a fostering couple is being reviewed, the RO can observe the quality of interaction between the couple as they discuss the fostering they have undertaken. It is important that anything of note observed by the RO, positive or concerning, is raised during the review meeting so that it can be explored and the implications for fostering scrutinised. The RO has the opportunity to note the quality of the foster carers' engagement with them as the RO, for example, how they were welcomed into the foster carer's home. The RO's observations are only ever snapshots of a particular day and should be thus contextualised within the review meeting discussions as well as within the RO's related report.

The RO sees the foster home at the review meeting and can form a view as to its appropriateness as an environment for foster children. They can note evidence of foster children's physical presence or the lack of it, the emotional warmth of the home and how the foster carer and their family are including a foster child through such things as displayed photographs and artwork. It is not the role of the RO to conduct a health and safety audit during the foster carer review. However, if the poor state of the home or the care of a foster child's bedroom has been raised in the paperwork, the RO should ask to see the whole house and the foster child's bedroom to inform their independent judgement. The RO should not rely on the assessment of the original assessor or previous ROs because circumstances can change. A key purpose of a foster carer's review is that the FSP satisfies itself that 'the foster parent continues to be suitable to be a foster parent and the foster parent's household continues to be suitable...' (DfE, 2011b). Brown writes that the judgements about the fostering household environment need to be properly discussed at the review meeting.

> *This professional judgement about the home as a suitable environment for a foster child is in addition to the health and safety checks, and the safer care policies for the foster children. It is more about such things as: the care taken of a foster child's bedroom, how individualised is it; what toys and/or equipment does the foster child have; where does a foster child do their homework...*

(Brown, 2014a, p109)

As well as making sure that the review meeting offers the opportunity for a holistic evaluation of the foster carer's work during the review period, any specific concerns must be explicitly addressed during the meeting. The RO needs to make sure that anything that might later be written in their report has been covered with the foster carer and the SSW. At the end of the review meeting, it is helpful for the RO to summarise the main areas that have been discussed, identifying the strengths as well as any concerns that have been raised. A plan should be agreed at the review meeting and set out in the review targets to ensure that any concerns are addressed and areas of development identified. Targets should include actions for the FSP, SSW and foster carer, identifying timeframes and responsible people.

If the RO, at the end of the review meeting, thinks that they will be recommending that the foster carer's approval be terminated, they can either tell the SSW and the foster carer at the end of the review meeting itself that they will be making such a recommendation or say that they are considering this but need to deliberate further through the writing of their report. If they decide to do the latter, it is incumbent on the RO to produce their report in a matter of days after the review meeting so that the foster carer is not left in a state of anxiety. If a RO is going to make a recommendation that a foster carer's approval be terminated, they need to explain the processes involved to the foster carer and ask that the SSW and the FSP offer further clarification and identify any necessary support (www.independentreviewmechanism.org.uk/fostering). The review meeting discussion and the material presented in the review paperwork inform the RO's recommendation regarding the foster carer's continuing approval and their terms of approval.

THE RO'S REPORT

The RO's report provides evidence of their analysis and synthesis of all the material that has been presented for the foster carer review. The report must draw from the review paperwork prepared before the review meeting and the content of the review meeting itself. At the end of the report, the RO must make a recommendation about the continuing approval or not of a foster carer and their terms of approval.

The RO's report must evaluate the quality of a foster carer's fostering against the relevant regulatory requirements. The RO's report should differentiate between fact and opinion and state specifically where information they are utilising in the report is drawn from; i.e. from the review paperwork prepared prior to the review meeting, from what was said in the review meeting, and/or from their own observations in the meeting.

After the review meeting has taken place, the RO must submit their report within a suggested maximum of three weeks to the SSW, the SSW's manager and the foster carer review administrator and wherever possible, sooner. Where the RO is recommending the termination of a foster carer's approval or a change to their terms of approval, the report should be submitted within a couple of days after the review meeting and should make reference to the role of the IRM if the FSP ADM is in agreement with the recommendation.

Having read the review paperwork and chaired the review meeting, the RO might have specific matters they wish to comment on regarding the SSW's or the FSP's practice. For example, they would need to comment if it had become apparent that the SSW visited the foster carer regularly but had not supervised the work of the foster carer but rather developed a relationship more akin to friendship than a professional working relationship. Or, for example, the RO might think that the FSP's practice contributed to a newly-approved foster carer's difficulties by placing three troubled young people with them leading to one placement ending chaotically. Independence from the FSP can help the RO make such observations. If the RO is drawn from the FSP, they ought to have a level of seniority or a role that enables them to make apposite comments in their report.

Whatever the structure of the RO's report, it should provide a properly evidenced, holistic, balanced evaluation of the quality of the foster carer's practice during the review period. The strengths of the foster carer need to be identified and examples given of what they have done well as well as raising any concerns and areas for further development.

Towards the end of the report there should be a discrete section that sets out the targets from the review for the FSP, the SSW and the foster carer. These targets should include development and training needs and identify timeframes as well as individuals who will take responsibility for each target being met. The final section of the RO report should set out the recommendation about the foster carer's continuing approval and their terms of approval with a rationale given for both. The RO might make additional recommendations, as was suggested in the Wakefield inquiry, regarding particular matters: 'The review could then have stipulated that there should be no further children placed with them until the matter was resolved' (Parrott *et al*, 2007, p83).

Currently, in England, 75 per cent of the looked after children population is in foster care. The quality of foster care matters for these children; the foster carer review provides the opportunity to enhance the quality of the care children experience.

> *It is therefore of great importance that, as social workers and foster carers, we garner collective passion and commitment to make sure that foster care is as warm, caring, and effective in meeting children and young people's emotional, educational, leisure, and health needs as it can be. Foster care can be, and often is the site of reparatory intervention, somewhere a child can recover, and move forward with hope. We have a responsibility to those children to make sure that their experience of foster care is as good as it possibly can be; providing the chance of, as well as recovery, fun, stimulation, new experiences, manageable boundaries, helpful routine, nourishment in all its forms, warmth and love.*

> (Brown, 2014a, pp141–42)

In requiring excellent foster care for foster children, we must remember that foster carers are human and fallible, as are we all, and that they and their families will experience changes of circumstances or particular difficulties, as all families do over time. This might mean that a RO recommends, in addition to a foster carer's continuing approval and terms of approval, particular requirements appropriate to the foster carer's circumstances. For example: that no foster child is placed for the next three months to enable a foster carer to settle into their new home and complete building work on their attic extension; or that no foster children are placed until the foster carer's own child's educational needs are met within their new school; or that no further foster children are placed until work is undertaken with the fostering couple about how caring for foster children impacts on the quality of their relationship and what the implications are of this on their care of foster children; or that the care of their own learning disabled son's new baby is planned and settled before another foster child is placed into their already busy foster family. Recommending that no further foster children are placed with a foster carer is not necessarily a criticism of them or their fostering ability but can be a realistic appraisal of what can be reasonably expected of a foster carer. Sometimes foster carers need to focus on their own family members' needs and/or the foster children that are currently placed with them.

When the RO's report is received by the foster carer review administrator, the SSW and the SSW manager, it should be checked for factual inaccuracies, agreed with the RO and then collated with the rest of the review paperwork. This final review documentation should then be signed off by the SSW manager as being ready and fit to be submitted to the FSP's fostering panel and/or the ADM.

SUMMARY

The foster carer review meeting offers the opportunity for the foster carer, SSW and RO to consider in detail and depth the quality of the fostering that has been undertaken during a review period thus enabling an evaluation to be made of the quality of that foster care. The review meeting is where differences of view, concerns and areas for further development can be explicitly discussed and plans made about how they will be addressed. The review meeting is a forum in which a foster carer's work can be appraised and where examples of good and excellent work can be identified.

'A successful, stable placement is central to supporting the needs of children in care. Carers are the centre of a child or young person's experience of corporate parenting and should provide the mainstay of their support' (DfES, 2007, p8). The foster carer review is the quality assurance mechanism by which the foster carer's central role in a foster child's lived experience of corporate parenting is evaluated. Its significance and importance as part of maintaining good quality experiences for foster children cannot be over-emphasised. The role of the review meeting is a central part of the foster carer review process.

8

Foster carer reviews and fostering panels

INTRODUCTION

Chapter 7 considered the role of the RO in evaluating the quality of the fostering undertaken by a foster carer in the review period. The RO makes a professional judgement in this evaluation, which informs their recommendation regarding the continuing approval of a foster carer and their terms of approval. Borthwick and Lord state that the 'purpose of the review is to provide an appraisal of the carer's abilities and experience of fostering over the year' (2011, p33). The fostering panel provides a further quality assurance process whereby the final review paperwork, which includes the RO's report, the targets they have set and their recommendations can be further scrutinised by the fostering panel. The fostering panel process adds another dimension to the necessary rigour needed to make sure that foster children are offered good quality foster care.

FREQUENCY

FSPs differ in the frequency that foster carer reviews are submitted for their fostering panel's consideration. First reviews of newly-approved foster carers have to be presented to fostering panels within a year of the foster carer's approval (DfE, 2011b). I have recommended that, in line with the Wakefield inquiry and Borthwick and Lord (2011), first reviews be conducted within six months of a foster child being placed with a newly-approved foster carer or within the year, since approval, whichever is the sooner.

Borthwick and Lord, writing about the role of fostering panels in relation to foster carer reviews, write:

The fostering panel is required to consider the first review of all foster carers ... This must have taken place within one year of approval... In addition, the panel may consider subsequent reviews if referred by the fostering service provider. It is also required to advise on procedures about how reviews are carried out and to monitor these.

(2011, p33)

The frequency of when these "subsequent reviews" are referred to fostering panels varies between FSPs. Some fostering panels see the review paperwork for every foster carer review. Others refer their foster carer reviews, after the first review, to the fostering panel every three years. Wherever possible and if resources allow, fostering panels should see *all* foster carer reviews as this is good practice. However, the realities of resource constraints mean that for many FSPs this is not possible. In this case, best practice would suggest that fostering panels see a foster carer's review paperwork every three years as a minimum. Fostering panels offer a quality assurance role and this role should be exploited.

Where there has been a significant change in the foster carer's circumstances, not warranting a new assessment but triggering a review being undertaken, such reviews' paperwork should be seen by the fostering panel. When a review has been undertaken because there are concerns about standards of foster care or where there have been child protection concerns, then again, such reviews' paperwork should be scrutinised by the fostering panel.

In Borthwick and Lord's guide to effective fostering panels, they suggest the following for when foster carer reviews should come to panel.

- *For first reviews, panels could consider reviews of new carers at six months and then at one year.*

- *All reviews, where changes of approval are required, could be referred to the panel.*

- *Reviews following child protection concerns or allegations made about standards of care provided by foster carers could be referred to the panel.*

- *Reviews could be referred every three years, even where there is no change, in order to provide some external monitoring and scrutiny of agency and fostering practice.*

(Borthwick and Lord, 2011, p34)

PAPERWORK

The review paperwork submitted to the fostering panel should be proofread by the FSP and signed off by the SSW's manager as being fit for purpose. The review paperwork, as noted in Chapter 5 as required by regulation, must include:

- the SSW's report;

- the foster carer's report;

- the views of all foster children placed with the foster carer (where possible in report form);

- the views of foster children's social workers for all foster children (where possible in report form).

Good practice would dictate that the following ought to be added to this list:

- the views of all foster children who have been in placement during the review period but have moved on (where possible in report form);

- the foster carer's own children's views (where possible in report form);

- the foster children's parent's views (where this is appropriate and where possible in report form);

- third party views – for example, from a foster child's school, nursery, health visitor, etc (where possible in report form).

FSPs collate their review paperwork in different ways and each will have a rationale. Here I suggest one way to collate paperwork which can provide a logical progression for the fostering panel member reading the review paperwork. I have reiterated the content of the foster carer review administration form for the purposes of clarity.

- The foster carer review administration form

- A cover sheet identifying all reports that should be part of the review paperwork and the page number where the report is to be found. If a report is missing, there should be an explanation as to why it is missing

- The foster carer's details

- A brief profile of the foster carer and their household

- The dates of the foster carer's approval, their fostering agreement and their reviews

- Their current terms of approval

- The minutes of the panel that considered their last review or their approval

- Any placements that were made outside the foster carer's terms of approval

- The dates of the SSW's visits to the foster home

- The dates of the SSW's supervision with the foster carer

- The dates of unannounced visit/s made to the foster home

- The dates of all statutory checks including the foster carer's DBS check and LA check

- The date of the foster carer's last medical

- A list of the foster carer's up-to-date DBS checked support network

- An up-to-date and accurate list of each of the placements that a foster carer has had since their approval. Placements since their last review could be emboldened or italicised. This list should include the name of the foster child's social worker and in the case of IFPs also the foster child's local authority

- A copy of the most recent health and safety report undertaken for the foster carer's home, including any related actions

- The most recent pet questionnaire where required

- A copy of the foster carer's current personal development plan including the training that they have undertaken during the review period

- A copy of the safer caring policy for the foster children placed and/or for the foster carer's household

- The targets set from the foster carer's last review and how these have been met

- Reports from all foster children who have been in placement during the review period

- The foster carer's own children's reports

- The foster children's parent's reports (where this is appropriate)

- Third party reports – for example, from a foster child's school, nursery, health visitor, etc

- The foster child's social worker's reports for all foster children placed within the review period

- The foster carer's report

- The SSW's report which makes a recommendation regarding the continuing approval of the foster carer and their terms of approval

- The RO's report which makes a recommendation regarding the continuing approval of the foster carer and their terms of approval.

It is helpful for fostering panel members' reading of the paperwork, their preparation for panel, and for the fostering panel's deliberations, for the finally collated review paperwork to have numbered pages.

Fostering panel members need to receive the paperwork before a fostering panel meeting in plenty of time for them to read the review documentation and prepare for the panel.

FOSTER CARERS, SSWs AND ROs COMING TO THE FOSTERING PANEL

In the spirit of working in partnership, inclusivity and valuing the contribution that foster carers make to improve the quality of a foster child's life, foster carers should always be invited to fostering panels where their review documentation is being considered. The foster carer, the SSW and the RO will have written evaluative reports for the purposes of the review and need to attend the fostering panel to answer questions that might arise from the panel's scrutiny of the review documentation.

The Chair of the fostering panel should make sure that the foster carer feels welcomed to the panel and that they are treated in a respectful way through the panel process. Many foster carers find attending panels daunting but this can be mitigated to some degree through the respect shown to the foster carer. Mehmet addresses this when she writes: 'It can be daunting to enter a room where there can be up to ten people waiting to see you, however, it is a clear responsibility of any panel, especially the Chair, to make your attendance as comfortable as possible' (2005, p22). It is incumbent upon the fostering panel Chair to thank all the contributors for the work they have done in preparing the review documentation and summarise the strengths of the foster carer.

The fostering panel must explicitly address concerns and areas for further development that are identified in the review documentation but the panel process must not try to replicate the review meeting. Where the panel feels that the review process has insufficiently dealt with particular areas, and because of this the panel cannot safely make a recommendation regarding the foster carers' continuing approval and terms of approval, then the review should be deferred to a future panel date. If this is the outcome, clear direction needs to be given about what further work the panel wants undertaken, by whom and by when, to enable a recommendation to be made. The minutes of the panel that pertain to the particular foster carer should be sent to the RO, the SSW and the foster carer.

PANEL RECOMMENDATION

The fostering regulations state that the FSP 'must on the occasion of the first review under this regulation, and may on any subsequent review, refer their report to the fostering panel for consideration' (DfE, 2011b, regulation 28 (5)).

Having securitised the review paperwork and had the opportunity to ask questions of clarification to the foster carer, the SSW and the RO, the fostering panel should be in a position to make a recommendation to the ADM. The FSP ADM makes the final decision, informed by the review documentation and the deliberations of the panel about whether or not a foster carer should continue to be approved and what their terms of approval should be. In line with the regulations, this decision needs to be given to the foster carer in writing (DfE, 2011b).

Where the panel is recommending a change to the foster carer's terms of approval and the foster carer is in agreement with this recommendation, the rationale for this change and the foster carer's agreement should be noted in the fostering panel minutes.

Where an RO and/or a SSW recommend that a foster carer's approval is terminated and/or their terms of approval changed and the foster carer is not in agreement with the recommendation, then the panel process outlined in Borthwick and Lord's *Effective Fostering Panels* should be followed (2011, p36). The foster carer 'should have read this report and should have been invited to provide their own observations in writing for the panel to consider' (Borthwick and Lord, 2011, p36). Having read the foster carer's review documentation and having had the opportunity to ask questions of those involved, including the foster carer, the fostering panel should make an informed recommendation.

In such circumstances, the situation necessitates that the foster carer be advised that they might want to bring someone to support them as their attendance at the fostering panel is likely to be stressful. The attendance of a support person should be agreed by the FSP and the Chair of the fostering panel. Where a foster carer does bring a supporter, the Chair needs to explain their role in supporting the foster carer but not speaking for them. Where a foster carer brings a solicitor with them, the Chair needs to explain to both the foster carer and the solicitor that the solicitor is there in the role of a support person and not as a legal representative (Borthwick and Lord, 2011, p36).

If the fostering panel decides to recommend to the FSP ADM that the foster carer is no longer suitable to foster or that their terms of approval be changed, and where the foster carer is not in agreement with this recommendation, this needs to be explained orally to the foster carer by the fostering panel Chair and adviser, as does the subsequent process, including the IRM. The minute taker for the fostering panel should record that this was done.

Where the fostering panel recommends to the FSP that the foster carer's approval be terminated, or that their terms of approval are changed and the foster carer is not in agreement but the FSP ADM is in agreement with this recommendation, Regulation 28 (7–15) has to be followed (DfE, 2011b) and the related amendments (DfE, 2013a).

SUMMARY

The fostering panel's scrutiny of foster carer review documentation adds another dimension to the necessary rigour that should be deployed informing decisions about a foster carer's continuing approval and their terms of approval.

Foster carers undertake complex and invaluable work with foster children within their own homes, and attendance at fostering panels, although usually anxiety provoking, can be an affirming experience. It is a forum in which their contributions to the lives of specific foster children and to the wider community can be recognised. This recognition of foster carers' work is important.

Fostering panel members need to hold in mind that their primary responsibility is to foster children. The UKNSFC Standard 23.2 notes that 'The panel's terms of reference stress a primary responsibility to act in the best interests of children and young people placed in foster care by the authority' (1999a, p62). The welfare of foster children has to be the paramount consideration in line with legislation in the UK.

9
Conclusion

Foster carer reviews are central building blocks to monitoring and improving the quality of foster care and in so doing the quality of experience for foster children. They are important. Some would argue that they are more important than the foster carer assessment as it is through the foster carer review process that evidence is presented about the actual rather than the hypothetical quality of fostering that a foster carer has undertaken.

Foster carer reviews, if done rigorously and analytically, establish whether or not a foster carer and their household remain suitable to care for foster children and if their terms of approval remain appropriate. This in itself is crucial for safeguarding foster children's well-being.

This guide has located foster carer reviews within their legal and policy framework. It has considered recommendations and findings arising from inquiry reports and serious case reviews as well as underpinning knowledge. The practicalities involved in foster carer reviews that are necessary for effective reviewing have been considered, including: the administrative process; information gathering; the review meeting and the foster carer review's relationship to fostering panels.

As well as being a central safeguarding mechanism, reviews offer the opportunity to focus on the development of a foster carer and how a FSP can facilitate that foster carer's work as well as their development. Reviews offer the possibility through the evaluation of a foster carer's fostering practice to praise them for the good work undertaken and the considerable contribution that they make to a foster child's life, their family and the wider community.

Good practice in foster carer reviews requires them to be holistic as well as focusing on necessary specific areas. The review has to take account of regulatory requirements and policy initiatives that impact on the review process. The most fundamentally important aspect of a foster carer's work (their ability to offer good quality care to foster children) must not be lost sight of in the attempt to cross all the regulatory Ts and dot all the standards' Is. The Munro review of child protection has some important messages for social work as a whole that are of particular importance for working with children in public care and foster carers. She writes:

> A dominant theme in the criticisms of current practice is the skew in priorities that has developed between the demands of the management and inspection processes and professionals' ability to exercise their professional judgment and act in the best interest of the child.

(Munro, 2010, p5)

Professional judgement is crucial in the evaluation of a foster carer's work. This guide has argued that regulations have to be abided by and rigour is necessary to enable effective reviews to take place. However, it is important to heed Munro's words about the over-bureaucratisation of child welfare.

> The reforms have driven compliance with regulation and rules over time, with social workers increasingly operating within an over-standardised framework that makes it difficult for them to prioritise time with children, to get to know them, and understand their feelings, wishes, and worries.

(Munro, 2010, p7)

Foster children must be the focus of reviews as their experience is what matters.

> I've been in care since I was six and one of the things that really bugged me and annoyed me about social workers is that they think they know how you feel and they say 'I know what you're going through' but they don't know what you're feeling. I think that everyone needs to listen properly to children and not make assumptions.

(Care Inquiry, 2013, p24)

The importance of the foster child's voice being heard as part of the foster carer review process cannot be over-emphasised. The foster carer review is centrally about the continuing assessment of what it is like for a foster child to live with a particular foster carer. The ability to make a foster child feel welcomed, valued, cared for, respected, safe, warm and comfortable are fundamental to "good enough" foster care. We are reminded of this from a young person quoted in *Care Matters* and the last words of this guide should go to that young person.

> I think a foster carer's personality is what makes a good foster carer. I am interested only in their kindness, understanding and commitment to me.

(DfES, 2007, p44)

References

Adams P (2014) *Undertaking a Foster Carer Review: A guide to collecting and analysing information for a foster carer review using Form FR (England)*, London: BAAF

Austerberry H, Stanley N, Larkins C, Ridley J, Farrelly N, Manthorpe J and Hussein S (2013) 'Foster carers and family contact: foster carers' views of social work support', *Adoption & Fostering*, 37:2, pp116–129

BAAF Assessment Working Party (1998) *Preparing for Permanence. Key Issues in Assessment: Points to address during the assessment process*, London: BAAF

BAAF (2014) *Prospective Foster Carer(s) Report (Form F)*, London: BAAF

BAAF (2015) *Looked After Children Statistics*, available at: www.baaf.org.uk/res/stats

Bachmann K, Blackeby K, Bengo C, Slack K, Woolgar M, Lawson H and Scott S (2014) *Fostering Changes: How to Improve Relationships and Manage Difficult Behaviour: A training programme for foster carers* (2nd edn), London: BAAF

Beesley P (2015) *Making Good Assessments: A practical resource guide* (2nd edn), London: BAAF

Borthwick S and Lord J (2011) *Effective Fostering Panels*, London: BAAF

Brammer A (2010) *Social Work Law*, Harlow: Pearson

Brandon M, Bailey S, Belderson P, Gardner R, Sidebotham P, Dodsworth J, Warren C and Black J (2009) *Understanding Serious Case Reviews and their Impact: A biennial analysis of serious care reviews 2005–07*, London: Department for Children, Schools and Families

Briskman J, Castle J, Blackeby K, Bengo C, Slack K, Stebbens C, Leaver W and Scott S (2012) *Randomised Controlled Trial of the Fostering Changes Programme*, London: National Academy for Parenting Research, King's College London/Department for Education

Brown H C (2014a) *Social Work and Foster Care*, London: Learning Matters/Sage

Brown H C (2014b) 'Foster carer reviews', *Community Care Inform*, available at: www.ccinform.co.uk/guides/foster-carer-reviews/

Brown H C and Cocker C (2011) *Social Work with Lesbians and Gay Men*, London: Sage

Brown H C, Sebba J and Luke N (2014) *The Role of the Supervising Social Worker in Foster Care: An international literature review*, Oxford: Rees Centre, Oxford University

Care Inquiry (2013) *Making not Breaking: Building relationships for our most vulnerable children*, London: Fostering Network

Chapman R (2014) *Undertaking a Fostering Assessment* (2nd edn), London: BAAF

Corby B, Doig A and Roberts V (2001) *Public Inquiries into Abuse of Children in Residential Care*, London: Jessica Kingsley Publishers

Coulshed V and Orme J (2006) *Social Work Practice*, Basingstoke: Palgrave/Macmillan

Cree V and Myers S (2008) *Social Work: Making a difference*, Bristol: The Policy Press

Curtis Dame M (1946) *Report of the Care of Children Committee*, Cmd 6922, London: HMSO

Department for Children, Schools and Families (2010) *The Children Act Guidance and Regulations, Volume 2: Care Planning, Placement and Case Review*, London: DCSF

Department for Education (2011) *The Children Act 1989 Guidance and Regulations, Volume 4: Fostering Services*, London: DfE

Department for Education (2011a) *Fostering Services: National Minimum Standards*, London: DfE

Department for Education (2011b) *The Fostering Services (England) Regulations*, London: DfE

Department for Education (2012a) *Training, Support and Development Standards for Foster Care*, London: DfE

Department for Education (2012b) *Training, Support and Development Standards for Family and Friends Foster Carers*, London: DfE

Department for Education (2012c) *Short Break Carers Supplementary Guidance for Managers, Supervisors and Trainers, Training, Support and Development Standards for Short Break Carers*, London: DfE

Department for Education (2012d) *Setting the Standards: Using the Training, Support and Development Standards with support carers*, London: DfE

Department for Education (2013a) *Assessment and Approval of Foster Carers: Amendments to the Children Act and 1989 Guidance and Regulations, Volume 4: Fostering services*, London: DfE

Department for Education (2013b) *Delegation of Authority: Amendments to the Children Act 1989 Guidance and Regulations, Volume 2: Care planning, placement and case review*, London: DfE

Department for Education and Skills (2004) *Every Child Matters: Change for children*, London: TSO

Department for Education and Skills (2007) *Care Matters: Time for change*, Norwich:TSO

Department of Health (1991) *Child Abuse: A study of inquiry reports, 1980–89*, London: HMSO

Department of Health (2000) *Framework for the Assessment of Children in Need and their Families*, London: HMSO

Department of Health (2002) *Fostering Services National Minimum Standards*, London: The Stationery Office

Department of Health and Social Services (1999) *Code of Practice on the Recruitment, Assessment, Approval, Training, Management and Support of Foster Carers*, Belfast: DHSS

Department of Health and Social Services and the Office of Law Reform (1995) *The Children (Northern Ireland) Order 1995 Guidance and Regulations Volume 3 Family Placements and Private Fostering*, Belfast: DHSS and the Office of Law Reform

Department of Health and Social Services and the Office of Law Reform (1996) *The Foster Placement (Children) Regulations (Northern Ireland)*, Belfast: DHSS and the Office of Law Reform

Department of Health, Social Services and Public Safety (2007) *Care Matters in Northern Ireland: A bridge to a better future*, Belfast: Department of Health, Social Services and Public Safety

Derbyshire and Nottinghamshire County Councils and the Southern Derbyshire and Nottinghamshire District Health Authorities (1990) *Report of the Inquiry into the Death of a Child in Care*, Derby: Derbyshire and Nottinghamshire County Councils and the Southern Derbyshire and Nottinghamshire District Health Authorities

Egan G (2009) *The Skilled Helper*, USA: Wadsworth

Ferguson H (2010) 'Walks, home visits and atmospheres: risk and everyday practices and mobilities of social work and child protection', *British Journal of Social Work*, 40(4), pp. 1100–1117

Gloucestershire Safeguarding Children Board (2008) *Executive Summary 0105 Mrs Spry – Version 2*, Gloucestershire: Gloucestershire Safeguarding Board

Hammersmith and Fulham (1984) *Report on the Death of Shirley Woodcock*, London: London Borough of Hammersmith and Fulham

Heywood J (1965) *Children in Care*, London: Routledge and Kegan Paul

Höjer I, Sebba J and Luke N (2013) T*he Impact of Fostering on Foster Carers' Children*, Oxford: Rees Centre, Oxford University

Holland S (2010) *Child and Family Assessment in Social Work Practice* (2nd edn), London: Sage

Home Office (1945) *Report by Sir Walter Monkton on the Circumstances which led to the Boarding Out of Dennis and Terrance O'Neill at Bank Farm, Minsterley and the Steps Taken to Supervise their Welfare*, London: HMSO

Husain F (2006) 'Cultural competence, cultural sensitivity and family support', in Dolan P, Canavan J and Pinkerton J (eds) *Family Support as Reflective Practice*, London: Jessica Kingsley, pp. 165–180

Koprowska J (2010) *Communication and Interpersonal Skills in Social Work, 3rd Edition*, Exeter: Learning Matters

Laird S E (2010) *Practical Social Work Law: Analysing court cases and inquiries*, Harlow: Pearson Education Limited

Lefevre M (2010) *Communicating with Children and Young People: Making a Difference*, Bristol: The Policy Press

Le Riche P and Tanner K (1998) *Observation and its Application to Social Work: Rather like breathing*, London: Jessica Kingsley Publishers

London Evening Standard (2007) *Sadistic Foster Mother's 19-year Reign of Terror*, – www.thisislondon.co.uk/news/articles-23389711 accessed 18.6.2010

Luckock B and Lefevre M (2008) *Direct Work: Social work with children and young people in care*, London: BAAF

Martin R (2010) *Social Work Assessment*, Exeter: Learning Matters

Mehmet M (2005) *What the Standards Say about Fostering*, Lyme Regis: Russell House Publishing

Milner J and O'Byrne P (2009) *Assessment in Social Work*, Basingstoke: Palgrave/Macmillan

Munro E (2010) *The Munro Review of Child Protection*, London: Department for Education

Parker J and Bradley G (2010*) Social Work Practice: Assessment, planning, intervention and review*, Exeter: Learning Matters

Parrott B, MacIver A and Thoburn J (2007) *Independent Inquiry Report into the Circumstances of Child Sexual Abuse by Two Foster Carers in Wakefield*, Wakefield: Wakefield County Council

Reder P and Duncan S (2004) 'From Colwell to Climbié: Inquiring into fatal child abuse' in Stanley N and Manthorpe J (eds) *The Age of the Inquiry: Learning and blaming in health and social care*, London: Routledge, pp. 92–115

Reder P, Duncan S and Gray M (1993) '*Beyond Blame: Child abuse tragedies revisited*, London: Routledge

Rotherham Safeguarding Children Board (2009) *Executive Summary of the Overview Report of a Serious Case Review in Respect of Child V (Female) and Other Children Placed by Rotherham MBC with Foster Carers Mr and Mrs A*, Rotherham: Rotherham Safeguarding Children Board

Rotherham Safeguarding Children Board (2010) *Executive Summary of Serious Case Review Mr and Mrs B (Foster Carers)*, Rotherham: Rotherham Safeguarding Children Board

Smale G and Tusan G with Biehal N and Marsh P (1993) *Empowerment, Assessment, Care Management and the Skilled Worker*, London: NISW/ HMSO

Stanley N and Manthorpe J (2004) (eds) *The Age of the Inquiry: Learning and blaming in health and social care*, London: Routledge

Sutton C (1999) *Helping Families with Troubled Children: A preventative approach*, Chichester: Wiley

The Fostering Network (2009) *Standards Needed to Bring Foster Care in Northern Ireland into Line*, Friday, 27 November, 2009 www.fostering.net, accessed 22.10.10

The Fostering Network (2010a) *The Skills to Foster Assessment. Applying to Foster: An applicant's guide to the assessment process*, London: The Fostering Network

The Fostering Network (2010b) *The Skills to Foster Assessment. Assessing Foster Carers: A social worker's guide*, London: The Fostering Network

The National Assembly for Wales (2003) *The Fostering Services (Wales) Regulations*, London: HMSO

The Scottish Executive and the Fostering Network (2004) *Code of Practice on the Recruitment, Assessment, Approval, Training, Management and Support of Foster Carers in Scotland*, London: The Fostering Network

The Scottish Executive (2005a) *National Care Standards Foster Care and Family Placement Services*, Edinburgh: The Scottish Executive

The Scottish Executive (2005b) *Getting it Right for Every Child: Proposals for Action*, Edinburgh: The Scottish Executive

The Scottish Executive (2009) *The Looked After Children (Scotland) Regulations*, Edinburgh: Office of the Queen's Printer for Scotland

The Scottish Government, BAAF and the Fostering Network (2010) *Guidance on Looked After Children (Scotland) Regulations 2009 and the Adoption and Children (Scotland) Act 2007*, Edinburgh: The Scottish Executive

Thomas N (2009) 'Listening to children and young people' in Schofield G and Simmonds J (eds) *The Child Placement Handbook: Research, policy and practice*, London: BAAF, pp. 63–80

Trevithick P (2005) *Social Work Skills: A practice handbook*, Maidenhead: Open University Press

UK Joint Working Party on Foster Care (1999a) *UK National Standards for Foster Care*, London: NFCA

UK Joint Working Party on Foster Care (1999b) *Code of Practice on the Recruitment, Assessment, Approval, Training, Management and Support of Foster Carers*, London: NFCA

Utting W (1997) *People Like Us: The report of the review of the safeguards for children living away from home*, London: HMSO

Wales Code of Practice Working Group (1999) *Code of Practice, Wales: Recruitment, assessment, approval, training, management and support of foster carers*, London: National Foster Care Association

Walker S and Beckett C (2010) *Social Work Assessment and Intervention* (2nd edn), Lyme Regis: Russell House Publishing

Warman A, Pallett C and Scott S (2006) 'Learning from each other: process and outcomes in the fostering changes training programme', *Adoption & Fostering*, 30(3) pp. 17–28

Welsh Assembly Government (2003) *National Minimum Standards for Fostering Services:* Cardiff: Welsh Assembly Government

Welsh Assembly Government (2004) *Children and Young People: Rights to action*, Cardiff: Welsh Assembly Government

Wilson K, Ruch G, Lymbery M and Cooper A (2008) *Social Work: An introduction to contemporary practice*, Harlow: Pearson/ Longman

Fostering and assessment titles

For more information or to order, visit www.corambaaf.org.uk